Herbert
an architect for the people
Simms

HERBERT SIMMS

First published in 2023 by
New Island Books
Glenshesk House
10 Richview Office Park
Clonskeagh
Dublin D14 V8C4
Republic of Ireland
www.newisland.ie

Print ISBN: 978-1-84840-910-1
eBook ISBN: 978-1-84840-912-5

British Library Cataloguing in Publication Data. A CIP catalogue record for this book is available from the British Library.

Set in Bembo Std in 12 pt on 16 pt
Typeset by JVR Creative India

Edited by Djinn von Noorden
Cover design by Niall McCormack, hitone.ie
Cover images clockwise from top left: Chancery House (courtesy of the G. & T. Crampton Archive); Henrietta House (courtesy of Gary Teeling); Herbert Simms (courtesy of the Irish Architectural Archive); Chancery House (courtesy of the G. & T. Crampton Archive); Women's Bathing Shelter at Dollymount (William Murphy, Creative Commons License); Chancery House (courtesy of the G. & T. Crampton Archive)
Printed by L&C, Poland, lcprinting.eu

New Island Books is a member of Publishing Ireland.

10 9 8 7 6 5 4 3 2 1

Lindie
Naughton

Herbert

an architect for the people

Simms

NEW ISLAND

'In natural beauty of situation in the dignity of its wide streets and Georgian architecture, few capitals can vie with Dublin. Only during the past 50 years has the octopus of thoughtless development and ill-designed buildings seriously threatened our city.'

– Manning Robertson, *A Cautionary Guide to Dublin* (1934)

Contents

Preface

While the cathedrals, museums, colleges, parks and imposing palaces of government are never to be ignored, the
more modest buildings where people live, shop and work
make up the true fabric of a living and thriving city.

Dublin certainly has its grand buildings, among
them the Custom House, the Four Courts, City Hall,
the old Houses of Parliament on College Green, Trinity
College, Christ Church and St Patrick's cathedrals, and
the Royal Hospital in Kilmainham. It also has magnificent gardens, most notably the Phoenix Park, but also
St Stephen's Green, the Iveagh Gardens and the Botanic
Gardens in Glasnevin. Yet in the eighteenth century,
when the city as we know it was taking shape, it was
the red-brick Georgian squares and streets, with their
accompanying gardens and streets of shops that gave the
city its unique character.

From the early twentieth century onwards, new
buildings continued to add style – and bring life – to city

streets later colonised by anonymous offices and chain stores. These handsome constructions, although clearly modern, show respect for the city's heritage and sympathy for the streetscape: they enhance rather than impose, unlike so many later edifices of lesser quality. Pause and look and you will notice the detail: a curve to the corner of the building, an arch, small balconies, even – in the case of one complex – a playful aviation motif.

Dubliners will have passed these buildings countless times; you'll find some of the best at Chancery Lane, Townsend Street, Henrietta Place and Marrowbone Lane. They've become as much a part of the city as the grander buildings. Yet these were practical buildings constructed not with commercial intent, but for housing Dublin's less prosperous citizens.

Public housing, or social housing, as it's become known, is not always renowned for the excellence of its design. Good architecture costs money. But in 1932 Dublin struck gold when Herbert Simms became the city's first housing architect at a time when Dublin Corporation was embarking on a much-needed campaign to clear the city's notorious slums. Simms' brief was to provide housing for the homeless in the form of apartment blocks, as well as 'cottage' estates on the expanding fringes of the city.

Simms did his best work from 1932 to 1938, six years spent in a flurry of activity. He was chronically short of money, materials and manpower; he was put under pressure by politicians, bureaucrats and religious leaders; he was forced to take shortcuts. Yet his best buildings were sturdily built, with an elegance that makes them instantly recognisable. They've survived far better than later social housing projects since demolished. Although occasionally threatened by thoughtless local councillors, many are now protected structures undergoing sympathetic refurbishment.

Simms and his team's meticulous work are proof positive that well-built social housing can add immensely to the tone and style of a city. Following his example were city architects in the 1950s who also deserve recognition. With thousands again homeless in Dublin, and a dawning realisation that a living city needs homes, shops and other small businesses at its heart if it is to survive, his work remains a touchstone and an inspiration.

1

The Move into the Cities

From the early eighteenth century Dublin and other urban settlements all over the world were developing into cities, continuing a process sparked by the break-up of the feudal system many centuries earlier.

With living off the land no longer possible for most, and the industrial revolution seeing what we know as 'work' moving from handicrafts in the home to paid labour in the factory, thousands migrated from rural areas in search of paid work in the makeshift workshops and purpose-built factories of the cities. Housing these incomers, most of them impoverished, became a serious issue.

In 1798 James Whitelaw, vicar of St Catherine's in the Liberties area of Dublin, had made a census of his 'distressed' parish, visiting every house, cabin and hovel. His graphic descriptions of city life were included in a two-volume history of the city of Dublin, published in 1818.

Inhabitants of the Liberties, 'by far the greater part of whom are in the lowest stage of human wretchedness', occupied narrow lanes:

> where the insalubrity of the air usual in such places is increased to a pernicious degree by the effluvia of putrid offals, constantly accumulating front and rear. The houses are very high and the numerous apartments swarm with inhabitants. It is not infrequent for one family or an individual to rent a room and set a portion of it by the week, or night, to any accidental occupant, each person paying for that portion of the floor which his extended body occupies.

A single apartment 'in one of those truly wretched habitations' cost between one and two shillings a week. Two, three or even four families could share a single room: 'hence at an early hour we may find from ten to sixteen persons of all ages and sexes in a room not 15 feet square, stretched on a wad of filthy straw, swarming with vermin, and without any covering, save the wretched rags that constitute their wearing apparel'.

Thirty to fifty people might be found living in a single dwelling: one house, No. 6 Braithwaite Street, contained 108 individuals. In the Plunkett Street of 1798,

32 houses contained 917 inhabitants – that's an average of almost thirty souls per house.

Whitelaw queried why 'slaughter-houses, soap-manufacturers, carrion-houses, distilleries, glass-houses, lime-kilns and dairies' existed in the midst of these teeming slums. He highlighted the 190 licensed 'dram-houses' in the Thomas Street area where raw spirits were sold at all hours. Drunkenness was universal, even on the Sabbath, while the area supplied the more opulent parts of the city with its 'nocturnal street walkers'.

A primitive approach to sanitation was a major cause of disease:

> This crowded population … is almost universally accompanied by a very serious evil – a degree of filth and stench inconceivable, except by such as have visited those scenes of wretchedness … into the back yard of each apartment, frequently not ten feet deep, is flung from the windows of each apartment, the ordure and filth of its inhabitants; from which it is so seldom removed, that it may be seen nearly on a level with the windows of the first floor; and the moisture that after heavy rains, ouzes [sic] from this heap, having no sewer to carry it off, runs into the street.

The landlord was usually 'some money-grasping wretch, who lived in affluence in, perhaps, a distant part of the city'. In one case the entire side of a four-storey house had collapsed. To the astonishment of Whitelaw, about thirty inhabitants continued to live in the ruined building and paid the landlord rent for the privilege.

By the end of the eighteenth century, Dublin's population stood at a figure of 172,000 and it was considered the second city of the British empire. Its inner-city slums were the result not only of industrialisation and political changes but of an over-supply of expensive housing by speculative builders, followed by the arrival of rural labourers looking for work and needing accommodation. At the time Whitelaw and his co-authors were writing their history of the city, the Georgian streets and squares, both north and south of the Liffey, were still 'spacious, airy and elegant', although the number of civil servants looking for such accommodation had declined and the middle and professional classes were fleeing the filth and degradation of the city for the newly-created townships of Pembroke and Rathmines. Pembroke was mostly owned by the Earl of Pembroke, while Rathmines was controlled by middle-class businessmen such as Frederick Stokes, an English property developer.

Little changed over the next few decades despite major political upheavals. In 1801, largely in response to the 1798 rebellion by the United Irishmen, Ireland was integrated into the United Kingdom of Great Britain and Ireland under the Act of Union, with Irish MPs voting their parliament into extinction and Catholics promised the prize of emancipation under the union. The promise was not kept. Robert Emmet's 1803 revolution was the final flicker of radical, urban-based rebellion: future rebellions would be led by a rural population protesting against iniquitous taxes and rents. Dublin's decline from second city of the empire to provincial backwater had begun. For the next 122 years its 400-odd parliamentarians, many of them owners of large estates in rural Ireland, would conduct their business not in Dublin but at Westminster.

In the years following the Act of Union, the elegant mansions in Henrietta Street, Gardiner Street, Dominick Street, Summerhill and Mountjoy Square on the north side of the Liffey, many of them relatively new, were abandoned. Sites bought for building purposes were left derelict. Property prices crashed: a house valued at £2,000 before the union was worth about £55 in the 1820s. When not taken over by the better-off lawyers and bankers, the larger mansions fell into the hands of speculative investors, who sold yearly leases in the properties to smaller investors; these then let out rooms for a weekly rent. According to one visitor to the city in 1822, it was not possible to walk in any direction for half an hour in the city without coming upon 'the loathsome habitations of the poor'.

Previously, the rich had lived in the main streets. Their employees, as well as the city's small shop-keepers, publicans and businessmen, lived in the lesser streets behind or, in the case of Dublin, in 'the Liberties'. As the name indicated, the Liberties was an area outside the city walls dating back to medieval times, which was not under the jurisdiction of the city. It later attracted wealthy merchants from the thriving weaving industries, as many of the street names indicate.

Following the departure of the wealthier and their middle-class entourages from the city centre, warrens of poorly-constructed buildings appeared down narrow alleys, lanes and stables originally designed to service the larger houses. From the 1840s onwards, housing of this nature was often demolished to make room for small factories and for the newly emerging railway lines and stations.

With no native source of cheap energy and no parliament in Dublin, Ireland's few industries were left unprotected and forced to pay high duties on essentials such as coal. While its breweries and distilleries continued to employ large numbers of workers – as indeed did the manufacturers of biscuits and mineral waters – the silk industry was wiped out because of the unrestricted importing of raw and dyed silk into Great Britain and Ireland. Not even a reduction in wages could save it, although in 1824, when the first steamer service between Dublin and Liverpool was established, the silk industry was still employing an estimated 6,000 people in Dublin, about half what it had been at its peak. That would drop to no more than thirty to forty by 1832.

With its native industries in crisis, Ireland became primarily a supplier of cattle and agricultural goods to Britain. Dublin and its environs became a place of passage not only for livestock but increasingly for people; the great harbour of Kingstown, now Dún Laoghaire, built in the 1820s, symbolised the start of a new era in Irish trade.

Britain, the first truly industrialised nation in the world, had created an empire reaching all corners of the globe and was, by any measure, the most powerful nation in the world at the time. Lured by stories of well-paid work in the factories of Manchester, Liverpool, Sheffield, Birmingham and Glasgow, the rural poor arrived in Dublin seeking to find their way across the narrow Irish Sea to what seemed to them to be the Promised Land. Many got no further; others, who managed to scrape together the money for a ferry ticket, failed to find work and returned to Dublin soon after.

Before 1840 only 353 houses in Dublin were described as 'tenements'; that is, a city house originally built for one family taken over by a landlord or 'house jobber'. He then farmed them out as one-, two- and three-roomed 'apartments' for the highest rent possible without in any way improving the sanitation or adapting them for occupation by multiple families. Although scattered all over the city, most of the worst tenements were concentrated in the Gardiner Street and Dominick Street areas near the docks, while in the Liberties, the alleys and lanes off Francis Street, the Coombe and Cork

Street were as crowded and filthy as ever. Of the 25,822 families living in tenements, a total of 20,108 lived in one room. As Whitelaw had found in 1798, one house could contain as many as ninety-eight people.

While not quite as bad as in Whitelaw's time, sanitation remained rudimentary – usually consisting of an ash-pit and a 'privy midden', which consisted of an outhouse connected to a dump for waste in the back yard of a building. Originally, it had simply been a hole in the ground. For most, a bucket secreted in a cupboard was the family toilet. Only in the mid-nineteenth century did 'water closets', using water to flush away human waste through a drainpipe for disposal elsewhere, become prevalent. In Dublin that 'elsewhere' was usually the River Liffey, where a spring tide could cause the sewer flaps to close. As a result, the drains backed up, causing sewer gas to seep into the cellars with disastrous effects.

Mortality rates were shocking. A report in 1845 found that over half of all children died before they reached the age of five and only one-third of the working classes lived beyond the age of twenty. Politics at the time offered no solutions. Beyond the provision of workhouses after 1830, social welfare in the modern sense did not exist. Almost all housing was privately rented and *laissez-faire* politicians argued against any measures that might hamper a wealthy individual's right to compete freely in the marketplace. Little notice was paid to the workers living in the tenements who helped create that wealth. With 'municipal socialism' and state intervention frowned upon, voluntary organisations attempted to provide basic housing and other amenities. Only when it became obvious that the vermin-infested slums were a breeding ground for infectious diseases such as typhus and tuberculosis, and for the cholera that could infect the wealthy as well as the poor, was public funding used to lay water mains and sewer lines. Workhouses for the destitute and debilitated were also funded.

With wheat and other cereals difficult to grow in Ireland's damp conditions, most families in rural and urban Ireland survived on a diet based on potatoes. In 1845 the potato harvest failed. In the resulting five-year 'Great Famine', one million Irish men, women and children died and at least a further million emigrated. Infectious diseases, rather than starvation, were responsible for most deaths. With the famine creating widespread homelessness, extra workhouses were built to cater for 250,000 people. The famine was followed by a free-trade era, which left Irish farmers unable to compete in the British market with cheaper produce from America, Australia and the Russian wheat belt.

Because living off the land was proving increasingly impossible, migration into the larger cities continued, swelling the ranks of unskilled labour. By 1849 the number of tenements in Dublin had risen to 5,995; by 1890 it would reach 9,760. A cholera outbreak in

1848 spurred the provision of single men's lodging houses, while some employers were building what amounted to social housing for their workers. Among them was Thomas Vance, a merchant, who built a low-rent 'model lodging house' along with baths for thirty families at Chapel Lane off Lower Bridge Street in the Liberties.

Some recognition of the farmer's vital role in feeding the nation would come later when local authorities built thousands of subsidised cottages – the first state-funded social housing in Ireland or indeed in any part of the British Isles. The urgent need for providing public housing in a similar fashion in the cities was largely ignored. For most property-owners, it was easier to stigmatise slum-dwellers as drunkards, thieves and prostitutes than to recognise a larger social issue which urgently needed redressing.

From 1850 Dublin Corporation, which had replaced the landlord-class, dominated City Assembly in 1840, took responsibility for drainage, paving, cleansing and lighting in the city. After 1849 nationalists would come to dominate all the city's fifteen wards, promoting their own interests as the owners of small shops, pubs and tenements. When conservative unionists became increasingly exasperated at the jobbery and corruption of the Corporation, they began moving out of the city to new suburban townships, where they could have some control over their immediate environment.

A critical problem for all property-owners were the local 'rates', a tax based on the 'rateable valuation' of the property – the rent that a tenant was prepared to pay to a landlord. This was paid to the local council for providing services such as mains water, road maintenance and refuse collection, or 'scavenging' as it was then called. For example, in 1873 a house in Gardiner Street was available for rent at £60 a year plus an additional £17 16s 3d in local rates. A downward general revaluation of property in 1852 had resulted in a loss of vital revenue which, until 1890, came to the Corporation through a Collector General. Many landlords were reluctant to improve their properties since that would increase their rateable value, while Dublin Corporation conspired to keep rates low for property-owners by economising on public services. It was a flawed system unrelated to the ability to pay.

In 1851 Lord Shaftesbury, 'the poor man's earl', had introduced laws giving local authorities in Britain the power to build and maintain public lodging houses. By now the 'housing question' had become a matter of public concern, thanks to the novels of Charles Dickens and pioneering work by social campaigners, among them Octavia Hill. Over fifty years, she restored and managed 15,000 properties in London. Hill believed that charitable work must begin by looking after the family and providing homes for everyone. A weekly visit to collect the rent allowed for broader contact with the tenants and an offer of help if problems arose. Hill turned the rough open spaces around the alleys and terraces into playgrounds, and fought against the overdevelopment of precious open ground in city centres.

Good sanitation was the key to healthy living in any crowded city. Under the Sanitary Act of 1866, local authorities could compel landlords to connect their sewerage system to the main drainage system and Dublin Corporation recruited a number of sanitary inspectors from the police force. Shortly before this John Gray, the chairman of Dublin Corporation's water works committee, came up with a plan to provide Dublin with a water and sanitation system fit for a growing city. Until then Dublin's water had come from the canals, which were in private hands. Gray proposed building a large, publicly owned reservoir at Vartry in Roundwood, connected to Dublin by a 4 km-long underground tunnel; a considerable engineering feat for the time. The scheme proved an outstanding success, winning Gray a knighthood after it was opened in 1863. Yet despite occasional successes, with only 8,000 or so of the city's wealthier citizens having a vote, the interests of property-owners were rarely threatened and few, if any, were forced to improve the condition of their tenements.

Under the Labouring Classes (Lodging Houses and Dwellings) Act, also passed in 1866, private companies or municipal authorities could apply to the Irish Board of Works for loans to cover up to half the cost of a housing scheme at just 4 per cent interest payable over forty years. An immediate result was the emergence of joint-stock companies set up to provide urban housing with share-holders entitled to a dividend of no more than 5 per cent. One of the first was the short-lived Dublin Industrial Tenements Company, founded in 1866 by a group of prominent Dublin businessmen and public-health campaigners. Among them was Dr Edward Dillon Mapother, who had been appointed Dublin's first medical officer in 1864. Its New Model Dwellings, a four-storey brick tenement block with fifty small flats on a cleared site at Meath Street, was designed to house 2,200 of Dublin's poorest. It swiftly degenerated into a slum every bit as dangerous and unsanitary as the tenements it had replaced.

With only £190,000 advanced by the Board of Works over twenty years, the Act had minimal impact. Equally ineffectual was the Artisans and Labourers Dwellings Act of 1868 (the 'Torrens Act'), which gave local authorities the power to take over and, if necessary, demolish unsanitary dwellings when landlords refused to repair them.

In 1872 the Local Government Board for Ireland was created, taking over the functions of the Poor Law Commissioners and supervising municipal government and spending from its head office in the Custom House. Making up the board were the chief secretary and the under-secretary, along with three permanent members, including a qualified doctor as medical commissioner. While the Board readily agreed to loans for public lighting, electricity supply, drainage, street paving and the Fire

Brigade service, it baulked at financing costly slum–clearance projects.

Clearly government needed a push and when 1,650 people died in a smallpox epidemic that lasted from late 1871 to early 1872, public alarm led to the establishment of the Dublin Sanitary Association, which included doctors, lawyers and businessmen. It lobbied successfully for the extension of the Artisans and Labourers Dwellings Improvement Act of 1875 (the 'Cross Act') to Ireland, which meant that, for the first time, government loans for clearing the unsanitary areas of their towns and cities were offered to local authorities. The act boosted urban reform, with Waterford the first local authority in Ireland to build public housing.

Although financing any slum–clearance scheme remained a problem for Dublin Corporation, after 1875 the Board of Works paid for purchasing and demolishing areas, laying new streets and improving sewers, lighting and water supply. Three areas initially earmarked for clearing were the Coombe and Plunkett Street areas in the Liberties, along with Boyne Street, off Westland Row, in the city centre.

In June 1876 Dr Mapother had recommended the demolition and clearance of 110 dwellings in a four-acre site of the Coombe previously occupied by textile manufacturers and tradesmen. When clearing it proved costlier than expected, the Corporation was authorised to borrow £24,000 to cover the cost of compensating landowners, the expense of demolition and the installation of sewers, lighting and paving on what were new 'streets'. Since the Corporation was not yet prepared to take on the burden of constructing housing itself, the cleared sites were handed over to the Dublin Artisans' Dwellings Company (DADC), a joint-stock company founded in 1876 and chaired by Sir Arthur Guinness.

In 1880 the foundation stones were laid for 210 dwellings: ninety-two one-storey, 114 two-storey and four three-storey houses in four different designs. Class A and B were of Portland cement concrete; Class C was fronted with red brick, while Class D had front and end walls of red brick and side walls in concrete. Each house had its own scullery, coalhouse, privy and private concrete yard. By 1893 all but eight of the houses were occupied; those without tenants were used as shops and for housing caretakers. Rents ranged from 3s 6d to 7s; not unreasonable at a time when labourers, porters and carters could earn between 15s to 18s a week, painters from 24s to 29s and craftsmen up to 36s. Unfortunately, the annual rent of £200 per acre that the DADC paid the Corporation came nowhere near covering the cost of acquiring the site and servicing the £24,000 government loan.

Next for clearance was a site in Plunkett Street, off Francis Street in the Liberties, with the acquisition handled by Dudgeon Brothers, a commercial engineering and surveying firm. Fifty-two owners had lodged compensation claims totalling £39,891 3s 11d. Of these, twenty-seven sold out for £9,565 while the rest were in arbitration. Dudgeon Brothers had argued that acquiring property by private treaty was generally less expensive than arbitration, but by 1887 the total cost of clearing the area had more than doubled to £31,000 and the question of excessive compensation became the subject of a Royal Commission. After it recommended no further private deals, an arbitrator was appointed by the Board of Works. When Plunkett Street was finally cleared, it was leased to the DADC for £133 per acre – cheaper than in the Coombe. A scheme of red-brick cottages with internal water closets and sculleries was built, providing homes for 320 families.

Around the same time a special committee began preparing a scheme for improving and disposing of the Oxmantown Estate in Stoneybatter. Originally an open area, or rough commonage, stretching from Church Street to the Phoenix Park, the estate had been leased by the Corporation to the Earl of Ormond for a period of 200 years in 1682. After that lease expired, sixty-four tenement houses in the streets around Barrack Street and Tighe Street to the south of the estate were cleared. They had housed 1,048 people.

In that area and others, the DADC was purchasing its own sites, starting in 1877 with a scheme of 1,200 houses. By 1914 it had a portfolio of over 3,300 dwellings, making it twice as productive as Dublin Corporation at a time when few private developers were building houses.

Among its early projects were small flats in central schemes like Upper Birmingham Street, where thirty-two houses and flats were constructed, and a four-storey flat block at Echlin Street, which was criticised at the time as 'barrack-like' by the *Irish Builder*; yet this block has aged well and is still in use. Another flat block was built at Dominick Street, while the DADC was also buying plots in Rathmines, Bray and Dún Laoghaire. The schemes, aimed at the better-off workers, freed up cheaper tenement accommodation for the poorest of working-class families.

More purely philanthropic than the DADC in aim was the Iveagh Trust, set up in April 1890. In collaboration with the DADC, the trust began its work at a site close to the Guinness brewery on the corner of Thomas Court and Bellevue. There it built two large three-storey red-brick blocks, providing 118 single-room flats. These soon became overcrowded.

Other philanthropic organisations and individuals providing housing included the Dublin and Suburban Workmen's Dwellings Company, the Industrial Tenements Company and the Earl of Meath. The Association for the Housing of the Very Poor, founded by Sir Charles Cameron, the city's chief medical officer from 1876, provided single rooms for working men. Railway and transport companies built housing for their workers: the Great Southern and Western Railway Company with 142 houses in Inchicore; the Midland

Great Western Railway Company with eighty cottages at Grangegorman; the Dublin United Tramways Company with a hundred cottages close to the tram terminals at Rathmines, Terenure, Donnybrook and Dollymount. Among the organisations taking over and renovating tenement buildings were the Alexandra Guild Tenement Company and the Social Service Tenement Company.

Looking after the truly destitute were organisations such as the Sick and Indigent Roomkeepers Society, founded in 1790, the Society of St Vincent de Paul, established in Paris in 1833 with Irish branches opening from 1845, the Dublin Mansion House Relief Committee and the Association for the Relief of Distressed Protestants. If all else failed, the despised workhouse was there to support the sick and the aged. Numbers using the workhouses increased in the 1880s and again after 1902 when building projects slackened off and unemployment became a serious problem. For those attempting to stay out of the workhouse, pawnbrokers took in over 4.5 million 'pledges' in 1906 alone. Providing the elderly and the out-of-work with some financial support were the Old Age Pensions Act (1908) and the Labour Exchange Act (1909).

Yet however well-meaning, the philanthropic organisations only scratched the surface of the problem, which was that the poorest of the poor could afford to pay only the most minimal of rents. A further problem for the Corporation was rehousing those displaced by its building schemes: the bleak, barrack-like exteriors of the early flat blocks recalled the hated workhouses and fostered an enduring view that flat living was inferior or short-term, and only for those who could not afford to rent a cottage.

On the political front, the fall of Charles Stewart Parnell and the culture of mud-slinging and backbiting that followed caused widespread disillusionment with politics. Since 1870 the question of Home Rule dominated Irish politics and, despite the support of the Liberal British prime minister William Gladstone, Home Rule bills were defeated at Westminster in 1886 and 1893. With no national parliament sitting in Dublin, Dublin Corporation took over its role as a debating chamber and became increasingly nationalist in tone. Practical issues such as housing the city's poor slid down the list of priorities.

Not helping the cause was the number of city councillors who were quite happy to own or partly own tenement buildings in the Dublin slums, often charging high rents for poor-quality accommodation. Joseph Michael Meade, a master builder elected Lord Mayor in 1891, owned property valued at £60,000, including tenements in Henrietta Street. Of the Corporation members who owned tenements in the early part of the twentieth century, Alderman O'Reilly had nine houses, Alderman Corrigan nineteen and Councillor Crozier eighteen; all the properties owned by these three were rated as third class, or unfit for human habitation. Yet because he feared having the tenants thrown out on the street, these buildings were reluctantly passed as fit by Sir Charles Cameron. All three received tax rebates for work on their properties, without any evidence that this work had been carried out. Ten other Corporation members owned or had an interest in one to three houses.

With such tacit exploitation of the system, it was little wonder that moves to clear the tenements were met with indifference at best.

2

Corporation Housing:
the first buildings 1877–1913

Since it had become clear that local authorities must pro-vide acceptable accommodation for the poor, Sir Charles Cameron proposed that the Corporation should start building the houses itself.

Cameron estimated that the Corporation could still make a small profit while providing 10,000 dwellings at rents of under 2s 6d a week, and an official from the Artisans and Labourers Dwellings Committee of the Corporation was sent to study the St Martin's Cottages scheme at Ashfield Street in Liverpool and similar schemes in Glasgow and Edinburgh.

Since clearing the existing slums only shifted the problem to the next-worst slums, the ideal solution was not only to clear vast areas, but to begin building replacement housing paid for by long-term loans. Once the houses or flats were ready, tenants would pay rents subsidised by the rates. Unfortunately, neither the rate payers nor the Treasury were prepared to underwrite housing for the poorer classes.

In 1884, with no private builders prepared to take on the job, Dublin Corporation reluctantly accepted the need to start building for those 'whom no company would attempt to provide dwellings'. Yet when it embarked on its first scheme at Barrack Street, now Benburb Street, the DADC's directors objected 'that the Corporation have determined on the further erection of classes of dwellings which cannot fail to compete unfairly with those erected by the company, as they are to be let at rents involving an annual loss to the rate payer. The effect must be to discourage private enterprise.'

Permission was granted for the block flat scheme to be called Ellis Court on land the Corporation already owned at Barrack Street. As the name indicates, the street was located beside an army barracks, in this case the Royal Barracks, just off the north banks of the River Liffey. With its brothels and disreputable public houses 'filled with the most abandoned crew of rogues and prostitutes', the street was considered a 'sink of physical and moral contamination'. Attempts to buy up the leases as early as 1814 had proved too costly and it was only after a number of the buildings crumbled away that the Commissioners of Wide Streets acquired the leases. After the quays were extended to Kingsbridge, an empty site remained between the barracks and the river.

For this site, the city architect Daniel J. Freeman designed three four-storey red-brick blocks providing mostly single- and double-roomed apartments, along with a few shops, for a total cost of £27,920. The design was based on the tenements built by the pioneering Glasgow Improvement Trust in Scotland. Access to the different dwellings was by means of well-lit, well-ventilated halls, stairways and corridors. All sanitary accommodation, water supply and dust chutes were located outside for hygiene reasons. Rooms were larger than those in similar buildings. Foundations were dug in 1884, with the buildings completed by 1887.

The largest block with seventy-three dwellings and fourteen shops was located between a proposed New Street (the present-day Blackhall Place) and Ellis Street. The other two blocks, on a separate plot between Ellis Street and West Liffey Street, contained a large single shop on the ground floor, forty-three dwellings of one and two rooms, and a men's lodging house with seventy-two beds and a wash house. Rents began at 1s 6d, or 4d a night in the lodging house. The shops, at an average rent of 10s a week, provided much-needed income for the Corporation. Unfortunately, because the standard of construction was poor, the buildings required constant remedial work. The street, renamed Benburb Street in 1890, remained a no-go area for most of the next century.

Bordering Dean Swift's 'Lunatic Hospital' at Bow Lane West, where the Corporation also owned the site, a scheme of eighty-six flats in two-storey cottages, along with five shops, designed by Arthur Dudgeon, was built from 1888 to 1889 with rent from 2s to 4s 6d. Attempted economies included the use of reinforced concrete floors and flat roofs.

Long earmarked for clearance was the notorious Bull Alley area between Christ Church and St Patrick's cathedrals where, unlike in the previous sites, Dublin Corporation did not hold the leases. Buying out the tenement landlords, who were given ten years of rental income, cost £14,421 8s 4d, which was about £3,000 more than expected. Even weekly tenants got their cut – they were paid half a year's rent in compensation. Among the landlords was Brian O'Looney, a lecturer in Irish language and literature and afterwards professor of Irish language, literature and archaeology at the Catholic University until around 1882. O'Looney, a persistent violator of the public-health regulations, owned four houses, bringing in an annual rent of £132. By the time the four-acre site was taken over by the Iveagh Trust, the total cost had soared to over £220,000, making it the most expensive redevelopment project in the city to date.

Around 1896 came a proposal from Charles McCarthy, installed as city architect after Daniel Freeman, for sixty houses of seven different classes, mostly two- and three-storey at Bride's Alley, which was close to Bull Alley.

The site, bounded by St Nicholas of Myra church and Werburgh and Bride streets to the east and by Nicholas and Patrick streets to the west, would provide accommodation for 128 families. Following an application for nine blocks of seventy-two three- and four-storey artisans' dwellings, it was further developed from 1900 to 1902. These dwellings were finally completed in 1911, eighteen years after McCarthy's initial proposal, by contractors H. & J. Martin following earlier work by two other contractors.

For Nicholas Street, McCarthy designed a group of eight west-facing, four-storey buildings providing sixty-four apartments. Further blocks providing sixty-five flats were built at nearby Ross Road. While they were relatively plain buildings in red brick, the window and sill designs, and the Dutch-style curved gables, echo the Iveagh buildings. Although the entire scheme provided 176 flats of two and three rooms, the exorbitant cost of the site, as well as expensive foundation work, meant that the rents were fixed at between 3s 6d and 6s 6d.

Initially the plan had included shops in order to provide some revenue for the scheme, but when the Local Government Board refused loans for building the shops, the planned accommodation became more modest. In 1914 the average weekly wage of a household in Bride's Alley was close to 27s – much higher than in most tenement dwellings – and poorer tenants could not afford the rent. Ultimately, the Corporation curtailed the scheme with part of the land sold to Lord Iveagh for swimming baths.

In an effort to cover its costs, Dublin Corporation began building mixed schemes that included a better class of housing differing little in style from those built by the DADC. At a Blackhall Place scheme of eighty-six flats and twenty-three cottages, designed by McCarthy, rents ranged from 2s 6d to 7s 6d, yet the higher rents did little to ease the Corporation's considerable financial problems.

Another McCarthy project was St Joseph's Place off Eccles Street, a notorious hotbed of criminal activity and wild living, previously known as White's Lane. In the scheme, built between 1894 and 1895, seven parallel rows of eighty three-room cottages were contained within a U-shaped perimeter avenue. Density was low at 160 people an acre and rents at 4s 6d a week proved too costly for labourers. Sir Charles Cameron noted that none of the new tenants had previously lived in the cleared site; the original tenants had moved to other tenement rooms in the neighbourhood where they could afford the rents.

After the Public Health Committee stressed the need to provide housing for 'labourers, porters, small dealers, pedlars, hawkers, charwomen, rag-pickers, night watchmen, the inferior class of seamstresses, sandwich men, etc', the Corporation acquired a two-and-a-quarter-acre site spread over the Montgomery Street and Mabbot Street area in 1900. Known as 'the Monto', the area was one of the largest red-light districts not just in Ireland but in Europe. As 'Nighttown', it featured memorably in the Circe section of James Joyce's novel *Ulysses*: 'Figures wander, lurk, peer from warrens. In a room lit by a candle stuck in a bottleneck a slut combs out the tatts from the hair of a scrofulous child.'

By 1905 numbers 51 to 70 Montgomery Street were demolished to make way for the Foley Street flats. Some saw it as a plot to clear out what *The Irish Times* described as a 'loathsome locality', while others doubted that any respectable family, however poor, would opt to live at such an address. In the new flat blocks, the Corporation proposed to house 580 families in 484 single- and eighty two-room flats with rents ranging from 1s 3d to 3s; all the flats came with self-contained sanitary accommodation. Like in other problematic areas, a caretaker was carefully chosen to supervise the day-to-day running of the flats.

As predicted, the development was shunned after it was completed in 1905. By 1911, with the units almost entirely uninhabited, rents were cut by half. Not even that could entice tenants, especially since the less salubrious inhabitants were upholding the area's notorious reputation by operating brothels and shebeens from their flats. By 1913 the Bride's Alley and Foley Street schemes had between them lost the Corporation over £70,000, which was half its entire deficit in the pre-war period.

One suggested solution to the housing crisis in cities all over Europe was to build not in the city itself but on its fringes, where sites cost less. Ebenezer

Howard, an influential English urban planner, was proposing 'garden cities'. His bestselling book *To-Morrow: A Peaceful Path to Real Reform*, published in 1898 and reissued in 1902 as *Garden Cities of To-Morrow* proposed a new style of collective living, blending the best of town and country. Howard's ideal 'city' of no more than 30,000 people would include industrial, commercial and residential areas as well as an inner 'ring park' and a 'green belt' circling the outskirts of the town. It would be owned and managed by the residents and financed by rents.

Letchworth in Hertfordshire, north of London, would become England's first 'garden city' and attracted much attention internationally, with visits from, among others, the Bolshevik leader V.I. Lenin, as well as Dublin Corporation officials. It was designed by Raymond Unwin, already developing a reputation as an urban planner. Although well-established cities like London and Dublin were unlikely to be entirely abandoned for 'garden cities', Unwin's more realistic plan for 'garden suburbs' would prove hugely influential, with their characteristic culs-de-sac and T-shaped closes, roundabouts to slow down traffic and a central 'commons'.

By the end of the century, the Corporation was declaring that it needed a loan of £500,000 to rehouse 10,000 of its poorest citizens at rents of less than 3s a week. It also wanted the power to encourage speculative builders to provide suburban estates, or, when necessary, to build these itself. With the cost of city-centre sites prohibitively expensive, councillors felt that the financial dilemma posed by the housing question could not be solved until the city's boundaries were extended, so bringing in more revenue through rates. In 1900 Drumcondra, Clontarf and Kilmainham were brought under Dublin Corporation control.

Building continued with a number of small housing schemes in the early years of the new century, among them fourteen cottages at Elizabeth Place in 1904 and fifty-seven cottages in Clontarf. In Inchicore, where a 13-acre site cost £320 an acre, which was about 5 per cent the cost of the typical city-centre site at the time, 333 cottages of three and four rooms were constructed between 1905 and 1912. For these modest houses, with doorways opening directly on to the streets, yards to the rear and little in the way of open public space nearby, rents began at 4s, rising to 7s 6d.

As the city grew, so did the Corporation. In 1900 it had employed around a hundred staff; by 1916, that number had increased to over 400 non-manual, full-time workers. A major part of its responsibilities was waste disposal, with a further 500 men using horse-drawn carts to empty over 20,000 city bins regularly. After the refuse was brought to the destructor plant at Stanley Street, specially constructed tipping wagons trundled along the tramlines at night to the Fairview slob lands, which, until 1925, was effectively the city dump.

The work of the Corporation was conducted in general session and by committees covering its main responsibilities – finance and leases, improvements, public health, waterworks, paving, cleansing, lighting and markets. Also in its charge were the North and South Dublin Union workhouses, the Richmond Lunatic Asylum at Grangegorman and industrial schools. Total running costs for the city in 1916 were £900,000 with accumulated losses of £2.75 million including £400,000 in unpaid loans for the housing schemes. Any attempt to increase the rates was met with vigorous opposition by the city's wealthiest inhabitants, including representatives of Clerys, Switzers, Arnotts and Dockrells, and the notorious William M. Murphy, owner of the Dublin United Tramways Company and, later, the *Irish Independent* newspaper. Its dire financial situation forced the Corporation to borrow either from the Commissioners of Public Works or privately from assurance companies, friendly societies and banks.

In 1903 a meeting in the Mansion House of the Dublin Trades Council, attended by Dublin city councillors and MPs, discussed building cottages on the outskirts of the city and providing cheap tram fares so that working men living on the fringes of the city could get to their workplaces without undue expense. William M. Murphy would hear nothing of it and remained implacably opposed to 'wasting' public money on housing, or on subsidising the poor. All Corporation housing schemes completed by 1906 showed a substantial financial loss, although cottages were proving more successful than flat blocks. Workers, especially those prepared to pay higher rents, aspired to live in a cottage.

In 1907 the Local Government Board suggested that, rather than building small schemes at irregular intervals, the Corporation come up with a long-term plan for building larger housing schemes. The cost of clearing the city slums was now estimated at between £3 million and £4 million, which was more than a hundred times the sum borrowed for acquiring the Coombe site in 1877. For John Redmond, leader of the Irish Parliamentary Party at Westminster, a state subsidy for urban housing came second only to Home Rule on his list of priorities and he gave J.J. Clancy, the Nationalist MP for Dublin County, the task of drafting legislation based on an urban subsidy and cheaper public loans.

The result was the Housing of the Working Classes (Ireland) Act 1908, commonly known as 'the Clancy Act', which extended the borrowing period to eighty years, along with a two-year delay in the initial repayment of capital to the Treasury. Under the Clancy Act, local authorities were allowed for the first time to issue compulsory purchase orders for 'unsanitary' buildings they wished to demolish. A small annual fund of £6,000 would assist local authorities in repaying loans.

From this time, local authorities were virtually the sole builders of rental homes for low-income households.

Yet, with the Corporation already deeply in debt, the piecemeal approach continued, with no overall plan for the worst areas of the city and the usual three- to four-year delay between adopting a scheme and completing it.

Although much diluted when finally passed, the Clancy Act had a positive impact. By 1914 some eighty of the country's 125 urban authorities had taken out loans for housing. These included Rathmines, Blackrock, Dún Laoghaire and Pembroke in the greater Dublin area. Dublin Corporation remained the largest single builder of houses, and a newly-established Housing Committee began work in February 1913.

Dublin's physical spread grew in the early twentieth century with the ribbon development of low-density suburbs speeding up. Building costs were relatively low before the First World War, which encouraged speculative building. Landowners on the fringes of the city sold to developers who then sold leases to builders, usually in small parcels, with some sites better than others depending on existing roads, drainage and other essentials. Most builders would construct a relatively small number of houses and, after selling those, move on to the next scheme.

From 1908 the Corporation was building cottages on cleared inner-city sites. The Local Government Board set standards of design: a living room of 150 square foot minimum; main bedroom 120 square foot, other bedrooms 80 square foot, and two-storey houses preferred.

Irish nationalists and labour activists were becoming more militant and after the 1907 elections, when Thomas Kelly and William Cosgrave, both Sinn Féin, were elected as councillors, they fought hard for their urban constituents. A resolution to let new dwellings for a shilling a week per room was passed, as was a proposal to make the dwellings slightly larger, allowing 125 square feet for the main bedroom. Each scheme would be provided with a small playground. By 1911 the cost of land in the city varied from £4,000 to £10,000 an acre.

The need to rehouse low-paid labourers and their families close to their workplaces remained a priority. Workers at the bottom end of the scale had few rights: no allowance was given for travel, little overtime existed and, in bad weather, they could be laid off with no pay. Yet for the growing numbers of builders and developers in the city, their work was essential.

Although subsidised housing was clearly necessary if the city was to be rid of its slums, the chief secretaries for Ireland – James Bryce from December 1905 and Augustine Birrell from January 1907 to 1916 – were opposed to such a move, despite representations from Dublin's then Lord Mayor Joseph Nannetti and John Redmond. Subsidies were disliked at national level because they broke the link between rates and local expenditure and, in the view of the government, encouraged waste by urban councils. On principle, Sinn Féin was rejecting any policy dependent on subsidies from

London. Housing policy found itself caught between three entities – Irish nationalists on Dublin Corporation, the British government in London and the Dublin Castle administration. Because tenement blocks in the city centre were unpopular with tenants and lost money, those in authority were leaning towards the idea of low-density suburban developments where rents could cover costs, so helping reduce the Corporation's considerable financial deficit.

The most tireless advocate of suburbanisation was Corporation councillor Coghlan Briscoe, secretary of the Town Tenants League, which was founded in 1904 with the aim of securing for urban tenants the legal and rent protection enjoyed by rural labourers. Briscoe, after representing the Corporation at the 1910 Royal Institute of British Architects' Town Planning Conference, recommended that the Corporation build a garden suburb at Marino, then mostly open fields. The plan had its origins in a call around the same time for the creation of a local garden city following the redevelopment of Fairview village and reclamation work at the nearby strand.

In 1910, a few months after the Corporation's Housing Committee was established, Charles McCarthy and William Cranwill Wilson, an engineer with the Corporation, went to England to study Port Sunlight, an Arts and Crafts model village built on Merseyside by Lever Brothers, as well as Raymond Unwin's garden-city design in Letchworth and the Hampstead garden suburb. On his return, Wilson began work on a design for Marino.

In 1911 councillors Thomas O'Beirne and Charles Travers travelled to Birmingham to examine the city's approach to working-class housing. The pair returned to Dublin, recommending that Dublin and indeed all Irish towns be developed along modern town-planning lines with more parks and amenities for their citizens. By then, 'town planning' had come to mean suburban-isation, particularly for urban areas blighted by the filth and noise of industrialisation. Yet unlike in Britain, most older Irish towns were suffering not from unregulated industrialisation but from economic decay. Conserving the historic old towns at their centre would prove a later challenge.

Still, from 1911 to 1914 came a determined effort to introduce garden-city ideals to Ireland, combining the views of the visionary Scottish urban planner Patrick Geddes with that of Raymond Unwin. The impetus largely came from Lord Lieutenant Lord Aberdeen and his formidable wife Ishbel who, in 1911, invited Geddes to visit Dublin with his Cities and Town Planning Exhibition. Geddes, although not an architect, was a pioneering soci-ologist with innovative ideas on urban design. With his wife, he had renovated a tenement block in Edinburgh and he considered radical slum clearances a disastrous blunder that failed to tackle the problems they aimed to solve. The exhibition, held from 24 May to 7 June 1911 at the Royal Dublin Society's headquarters in Ballsbridge, attracted an enormous 116,000 visitors.

For those with an interest in public housing, it proved a busy year. The Royal Institute of Public Health held its annual congress in August, with 'Housing of the Working Classes' one of its themes, while in September, the Housing and Planning Association of Ireland (HAPAI) was established. Dublin Corporation councillor E.A. Aston, city architect Charles McCarthy and Peter Cowan of the Local Government Board were all founding members with Lady Aberdeen elected its first president. A year later, in October 1912, HAPAI held a Housing and Town Development Conference and from this emerged the Association of Municipal Authorities founded specifically to agitate for an urban housing subsidy. At the time, the third Home Rule Bill, introduced by the Liberal prime minister H.H. Asquith in April 1912, was making slow progress through parliament.

The year 1913 proved pivotal, with the bitter and prolonged lock-out of workers creating volatile conditions that would prepare the ground for the 1916 Rising. At the root of the problem was the increasing militancy of unskilled workers. These had joined James Larkin's Irish Transport and General Workers Union in their thousands, despite a threat of instant dismissal from their employers for so doing.

On 15 August the first workers to strike were dispatch boys employed by the *Irish Independent* newspaper, by then owned by William M. Murphy, a man implacably opposed to Larkin. He responded by 'locking out' all employees who had joined the union. Eason, the news-agents who carried the Murphy newspapers, then went on strike in sympathy, followed by dockers, who refused to handle any goods coming to or from Eason's. On 26 August, the opening day of the Dublin Horse Show, 700 tram drivers and conductors downed tools. Dublin came to a standstill. Tensions continued to rise and, at a banned mass meeting in O'Connell Street on Sunday 31 August addressed by Larkin, 433 ended up in hospital while countless others were injured by baton-charging policemen. Two men, James Nolan and John Byrne, died.

On the evening of Tuesday 2 September, two days after the riots in O'Connell Street, tenement buildings at numbers 66 and 67 Church Street, occupied by sixteen families, collapsed. The area had already been marked out for clearance. Fifteen people were trapped in the rubble; seven died and at least seven more were seriously injured. One of the dead was seventeen-year-old Eugene Sammon, who had managed to save six members of his family before losing his life in an attempt to reach his four-year-old sister Elizabeth. Sammon was a union member locked out of Jacob's biscuit factory.

Two months earlier Mrs Margaret Ryan, the owner of the houses, had been ordered by Michael Derham, Dublin Corporation's Inspector of Dangerous

Buildings, to fix a beam across the back room in No. 66 and a pier between the two houses. At the inquest into the tragedy, she claimed she had made the repairs to the satisfaction of the inspector and denied rumours of a 'connection' with Corporation officials. Later, Mrs Ryan would claim £677 in compensation for a cottage and tenement acquired by the Corporation; she was awarded £43 18s.

Pressure on the Corporation to clear tenements and provide housing for the poorer classes increased after the appalling tragedy. It had followed earlier tenement collapses in Townsend Street in 1902, with one death and several injuries, and in 1911 at North Cumberland Street, where two died after twenty-six notices were served. At a site on North King Street and Church Street, also in 1911, tenants had already been evicted when the building collapsed, although one man working on the demolition was killed. All over the city, walls were shored up with baulks of timber and around 600 buildings were in a parlous state. Streets were pockmarked with cleared sites waiting for redevelopment.

In November of that year the Local Government Board launched an inquiry into the circumstances of the Church Street tragedy, presided over by Charles H. O'Conor. The commissioners, led by Charles Travers, chief inspector of the sanitary staff, interviewed seventy-six witnesses in seventeen days and also visited the tenements.

In its report of the inquiry published in 1914, the authors examined the circumstances leading up to the tragedy. The 1911 census had shown that the city's population had grown by 20,000 since 1891, with 87,000 living in tenements and only 2,600 dwellings built in that period. Almost 10,000 men, women and children were living in housing that was in 'an advanced state of decay' and did little more than provide them with a roof over their heads. Most of the older buildings in Dublin were crumbling away, not helped by the vibrations of increased and heavier traffic. In their original construction, timber beams were inserted in the body of the walls, and as these rotted away, the walls weakened and bulged. If subject to vibration, the walls could collapse.

Of the 25,822 families living in tenements, 20,108 lived in one room. Sanitation was of the most rudimentary kind, consisting of a tap in the yard and maybe a water closet toilet. It was not uncommon to find human excreta 'scattered around the yard and on the floors of the closets and … even in the passages of the house itself'. Not all tenements were in a decayed state. Some 1,516 were considered 'first class', which meant structurally sound, although still vastly overcrowded.

In 1914 over a quarter of Dubliners were in pressing need of support; 6,600 paupers were getting 'indoor relief' in Dublin's two workhouses, while a further 11,000 were getting 'outdoor relief', which consisted of a portion of bread, tea and sugar distributed every Tuesday and Thursday. A majority of these citizens were suffering from malnutrition, with children stunted in growth and prone to illnesses such as rickets and scurvy.

Repairing and restoring the best of the tenements could house 13,000 families, leaving a minimum of 13,958 dwellings required elsewhere. The inquiry was in favour of moving slum-dwellers to new estates on the outskirts of the city; that could even include 'some of the work-shy and loafing class' who should more properly be dealt with under a reformed Poor Law system.

Patrick Geddes, brought over by Lady Aberdeen and the Women's National Health Association to contribute to the inquiry, remarked that the poor were often treated 'as if they were mere passive creatures to be housed like cattle'. State aid should concentrate on rehousing the 'submerged' 10 per cent in well-built houses with a social mix in the city centre, even as the suburbs grew. Geddes supported the idea of refurbishing suitable buildings; that same year Sir Charles Cameron was warning that Gardiner Street was turning into a street of tenements and suggested that the Corporation acquire them. He was strongly opposed by the city architect, Charles McCarthy.

Perhaps because it was commissioned by the Local Government Board, the inquiry did not examine the political aspects of the housing crisis too closely, although it did acknowledge that the Corporation's chronic lack of money was the greatest obstacle it faced in attempting to solve the problem. A situation that had developed over seventy years was unlikely to be remedied in one or two years.

'Even if it were possible, it would not be desirable to seek to cure it in one or two years. Nothing would … be so detrimental to the best interests of the city, or more likely to attract a further population to the city than hasty and indiscriminate building of dwellings for the working classes,' said the report.

The authors concluded that any scheme for housing reform 'must ultimately contemplate the complete breaking up of the tenement system' with every working family entitled to a 'self-contained dwelling of sufficient size to prevent overcrowding, and which admits of the separation of the sexes'.

The Corporation was asked to come up with a plan for building 14,000 new homes and the complete abolition of the tenement system within two years. One problem was the Liberal government, which was ignoring the problems of chronic unemployment and casual labour not only in Ireland but in the overcrowded cities of industrial Britain.

A memorandum at the end of the report written by J.F. McCabe warned that 'past schemes of the Corporation show little conformity with modern ideas. They have looked to a part and not to the whole of the city. The maximum number of houses has been put on each site and the resulting density of population perpetuates slum conditions.'

A civic survey was vital. 'A Civic Survey embraces all the factors hitherto left out of consideration – the topography, the means of communication, the industries (past, present and future) and the movements, needs and occupations of the population of Dublin and its surroundings.' McCabe concluded: 'To build without a town plan in the old city will prevent effectively Dublin ever becoming what it should be – as beautiful as its own surroundings.'

3

A Grand Plan for Dublin:
1914–30

With the First World War, the 1916 Rising and the War
of Independence, followed by the creation of the Irish
Free State and a bitter and bloody civil war, the decade
from 1914 to 1924 was to prove turbulent both for
Ireland and Dublin.

During the war some 200,000 Irish men and women
joined the British forces, providing many Dublin families with a steady income for the first time in their lives.
Thanks to the demand in Britain for Irish agricultural
products, the economy was booming, although for the
poor, still mostly living in tenement housing, it made little difference. Adding to their misery were coal shortages
and inflated food prices.

When Herbert Samuel, the president of the Local
Government Board from February 1914 to May 1915,

proposed an ambitious plan for clearing the slums, he was forced to backtrack. He had argued that '... the greatness of Dublin depends not only on noble thoroughfares and palatial public buildings but also in no less a degree on the provision of comfortable sanitary homes for the population ... It is of the first importance to provide for the health and comfort of the people; it is only a secondary object to make a noble and archi-tecturally fine city.'

Despite those sound sentiments, the London-based Treasury feared that if Dublin was granted urban housing subsidies, every city in Britain would demand the same level of support.

In January 1914 the Aberdeens, prompted by Patrick Geddes, came up with two more town-planning ini-tiatives – a Civic Exhibition and a Dublin Town Plan competition. John Nolen, a leading US planner, was appointed manager of the exhibition, which would pro-mote the American 'City Functional' idea. Its central belief was that town planning was essential if cities were to function effectively. In April of that year the Citizens' Housing Council, which was promoting garden suburbs, offered the services of Geddes and Raymond Unwin to the Corporation's Housing Committee as advis-ers. Although the Corporation still favoured inner-city housing schemes, the offer was accepted.

A report, written mainly by Unwin, again proposed a garden suburb for Marino, with Frank Mears, Geddes' assistant and son-in-law, helping with the design. Unwin and Geddes were keen to stress that their 'town-planning' ideas should not be seen as a solution to the general problem of poverty. Still, if the Corporation built high-standard garden suburbs for artisans who could afford to pay the higher rents, the inner-city dwellings they left behind could be used for housing the very poor. The report was dismissed by the Corporation which, despite the ongoing demands for Home Rule, wanted the British government to subsidise housing for the very poor in Ireland.

Although a world war was looming, the Town Planning Competition and Exhibition took place at Linenhall buildings and the Temple Gardens in the King's Inns grounds from 15 July to 31 August, attracting 9,000 visitors on its opening day alone. Centrepiece was the cities and town planning show put on by Geddes, which documented the evolution of cities throughout the world, including a detailed survey of Edinburgh, and the beginnings of a civic survey for Dublin.

Before the exhibition ended, Dublin Corporation confirmed Geddes and Unwin as consultants to a number of its proposed housing schemes. After looking over the plans for Fairbrothers' Fields, Faussagh Lane in Cabra and Marino, as well as others planned for Beresford Street, Church Street and Ormond Market, Geddes and Unwin recommended a lower density of housing. They also argued that building on small plots

49

in the city centre, such as at Ormond Market, would merely increase the value of the adjacent land.

Central to the exhibition was the competition to draw up a comprehensive new town plan for Dublin, sponsored by the Civic Institute of Ireland. Geddes had persuaded Lord Aberdeen to give a generous £500 prize for the winning entry, which meant that the competition attracted the attention of architects all over Britain and Ireland. In all, eight plans were submitted. Judging them would be Geddes, Charles McCarthy and John Nolen. On 28 July the First World War was declared and everything was put on hold, including grandiose plans for reshaping Dublin city.

It took well over a year before the assessors finally met and only in 1916 was a plan submitted by Patrick Abercrombie, with collaborators Sydney Kelly and Arthur Kelly, declared the winner. Abercrombie, appointed professor of civic design at Liverpool University in 1915, saw Dublin as 'a city of magnificent possibilities containing features of the first order but loosely related and often marred by the juxtaposition of incongruities and squalor'. Dublin, he famously commented, had 'the most architectural slums in Europe'.

Abercrombie's plan aimed to create a new centre to the city, grouping together the industrial areas, providing new housing in the suburbs with road links to the city, and creating a system of urban parks and playgrounds. He proposed re-engineering the city around two main thoroughfares punctuated by buildings in the classic style; a style pioneered by Georges-Eugène Haussmann when rebuilding Paris between 1853 and 1870.

Because a derelict site in the city centre now cost £4,070 an acre, and existing housing in the city was scattered, Abercrombie suggested moving over a thousand families to housing on the fringes of the city. Yet he was no fan of what he called the 'machine-made monotony' of the typical new suburb; he cited as an example the 'dreary rows of twenty houses' built by Dublin Corporation in Inchicore, with small gardens and nowhere for children to play. 'The prospects for the future of a city on these lines is dismal,' he wrote. He suggested preserving existing tenement buildings by knocking three large houses into one, retaining the central staircase and converting the other two stairways into sanitary blocks. In his view, these beautiful buildings with 'spacious rooms, simple architecture, dignified doorways and ample sash windows' were worth saving.

For dockers and city-centre workers, Abercrombie came up with a scheme of self-contained houses and tenements that could house 3,698 people in the area around Townsend Street; this would include spaces for recreation and a children's play area. Among his other proposals were the reclamation of Dublin Bay on the north side, an underground railway network and the siting of the City Offices at Wood Quay.

With war raging in Europe and political upheaval in Ireland, the proposal, called *Dublin of the Future*, remained unpublished until 1922 when it was officially endorsed by Horace Tennyson O'Rourke, who would replace McCarthy as city architect in 1921. It would influence Dublin housing policies for decades, with a slimmed-down version called *Sketch Plan for Dublin* appearing in 1941. By then, Patrick Abercrombie was the most celebrated town planner of his generation.

Dublin Corporation had continued with its building plans before war struck. Two schemes completed by 1914, at Cook Street and at Linenhall on Lurgan Street, provided ninety-four single-storey 'cottage' dwellings. For the Linenhall scheme, close to the disused barracks, the slums on Coleraine and Lurgan streets were cleared. Slums in Beresford Street, Church Street, Spitalfields and Ormond Market were next on the list for clearance and development and, in April 1915, the Corporation put in a request to the Local Government Board for a further £31,980 for the Beresford Place/Church Street scheme. Since funding was scarce because of the war effort, Peter Cowan, now the board's chief housing officer, suggested that the Corporation borrow on the open market for future housing schemes. With thousands of men leaving for the war front in northern France and for well-paid munitions work in Britain, fewer rental houses were needed in Dublin, although many tenement buildings in shocking condition remained inhabited. 'The trenches are safer than the Dublin slums' was how one army recruiting slogan baldly put it.

All changed radically after Easter 1916, when a small group of Irish rebels took over the General Post Office and other large buildings in Dublin's city centre. Although the rebellion was crushed within six days, the brutal manner in which the British military executed the insurrection's leaders and destroyed the city centre with heavy bombardment had lasting repercussions. Although some £2.5 million-worth of damage was done to buildings, grants of only £1.75 million were made available for the reconstruction of O'Connell Street and the surrounding areas, which had been reduced to rubble. Miraculously, the nearby city-centre tenements remained untouched, to the chagrin of many.

As George Bernard Shaw put it: 'Oh why-o-why didn't the artillery knock down half Dublin while it was at it? Think of the insanitary areas, the slums, the glorious chance of making a clean sweep of them … I'd have laid at least 17,900 of them flat and made a decent town of it!'

In the aftermath of 1916, Augustine Birrell, the well-intentioned chief secretary, resigned and was replaced by Henry Duke, a pragmatic unionist barrister. Dublin Castle had decided that the best way to control Irish disaffection was by addressing the obvious need for better urban housing, and Duke's first public engagement was to open Pembroke Urban District Council's housing estate at Stella Gardens in Ringsend, designed by George

O'Connor. A special housing loan made to Dublin
Corporation was intended to calm political opposition
in Ireland and to pave the way for conscription at a critical point in the war.

Blocks providing forty-eight flats, as well as a number
of cottages, at Moss Street, Luke Street and Townsend
Street in the Trinity Ward, were built by 1917, as were
146 cottages in Church Street. Long-delayed work began
on the Ormond Market scheme at a site off the north
quays beside the fruit and vegetable markets. It would
take four years to complete.

Objecting to McCarthy's intention to resuscitate
the Ormond Market plan were Unwin and Geddes,
who argued that a more distinguished building, such
as a cathedral, would be more appropriate for a site
so close to the Four Courts. McCarthy, supported
by Thomas Kelly, the chairman of the Corporation's
Housing Committee, won out. Both believed that
fringe housing would never suit the poorest of slum-
dwellers, who lived in tight-knit communities and
relied on their neighbours in the struggle to survive. Since few households brought in more than £1
a week, a rent of two shillings was as much as they
could afford. For his part, the redoubtable Sir Charles
Cameron, still the city's chief medical officer at the
age of eighty-three, argued that no local-authority
housing should cost more that 3s 6d a week and that
flats with weekly rents of between 1s and 1s 6d were

desirable. If all the working class could afford to pay 4s 6d in rent, there would be no slums, he pointed out.

In late 1917 Henry Duke asked Peter Cowan to prepare a confidential memo on Dublin's housing needs. Cowan recommended building 16,500 new houses in Clontarf, Drumcondra, Cabra and Crumlin of sufficient size to allow for separating the sexes and with scullery and water closet. Yet a North City survey conducted in 1918 found tenants making it clear that their first choice for accommodation would be a refurbished flat in an existing tenement. Next preference was a centrally located cottage, with a suburban home only coming in third.

Cowan proposed that a further 13,000 dwellings could be provided by remodelling 3,803 first- and second-class tenement houses in flats of one to four rooms. In all, his plan was to house 27,000 families, which was the figure accepted by a Departmental committee four years earlier. Since then, 936 tenement dwellings housing 3,989 families had been cleared by the Corporation. In the same period, just 327 new houses were built on the fringes of the city. Overall cost was £8.64 million. Because it was dominated by tenement-owning councillors, Cowan felt that the Corporation was not fit to carry out such work and proposed the establishment of a Dublin Housing Board, subsidised short-term by the state.

Ironically, the design for Ormond Market came from Horace O'Rourke, appointed as McCarthy's assistant architect in 1918, who favoured garden-suburb ideals. A year later the plan was approved. After winning the contract, builders H. & J. Martin began constructing 128 dwellings around a landscaped square, using skilled craftsmen and traditional materials – yellow brick, slate roofs and timber windows and doors. Built as terraces, the houses had either three or four rooms, while the flats had two rooms. Each dwelling had an internal water closet, scullery and water supply. The combination of family homes and flats was progressive, catering for the mixed population found living around the markets.

Apart from Ormond Market, other proposed schemes included 234 houses at Mount Brown, close to the walls of the South Dublin Union; 694 houses on a largely agricultural tract of land in the Liberties at Fairbrothers' Fields; and a scheme for 232 flats at Glorney's Buildings in Summerhill. While the Local Government Board refused a loan for Glorney's Buildings, the other schemes were completed between 1917 and 1927, providing 1,140 of the planned 1,700 dwellings. In 1919 a scheme of ninety flats was proposed for Crabbe Lane, off Mercer Street, but the plan was delayed, only resurfacing a few years later.

While events such as a Civic Week in 1917 were promoting suburban housing for the working classes, the Corporation made it clear that it intended to continue with inner-city schemes like Spitalfields in the Liberties, as well as with inner-suburbs projects at the McCaffrey Estate and Fairbrothers' Fields sites, which would be built on garden-suburb lines. After negotiations with Chief Secretary Duke and the Local Government Board, it received a £100,000 advance to start work.

By June 1917, realising that it had underestimated the financial effects of wartime inflation, the Corporation requested that post-war housing subsidies be retrospectively granted. When the request was turned down, it opted to build only at Spitalfields. Although it would finalise the sale and clearing of other sites, it would not start building on them until a state subsidy was confirmed. In May 1918, after Dublin Castle pointed out to the Corporation that only £44,000 of the £100,000 advance had been taken up, work reluctantly began on the McCaffrey estate and on a small scheme at St James's Walk, also known as Colbert's Fort, in Rialto.

The McCaffrey scheme (later Ceannt Fort) of 202 four-room houses was initially sketched out by Charles McCarthy in early 1915. Density was twenty-nine to the acre, which was much lower than in previous Corporation schemes. Two children's playgrounds were provided. Once a grant was approved, Thomas Byrne was brought in as architect. He took an Arts and Crafts approach to the seven-acre site, and the terraced housing was built in yellow brick with a stepped roof line, punctuated by hips and gables. With an indoor toilet downstairs, the Corporation was designing at a higher level than previously, yet while the design was praised, the rent was set at 7s a week, which belied the Corporation's supposed commitment to providing cheap housing for unskilled labourers in the city centre.

At Spitalfields and at Church Street, two plainer house designs were used, with a greater variety of brickwork the only innovation. These schemes were bitterly opposed by the Citizens' Housing Council and by the newly-formed Dublin Tenants' League, set up by James Larkin's brother William, who favoured suburban development.

Housebuilding in 1918 was proceeding at about a quarter of the 1909 level, with the Treasury constantly undermining and frustrating the Corporation's plans, such as the clearance of Boyne Street in early 1918. At the time, the British Cabinet was more concerned with persuading – or coercing – Irishmen to enlist in the armed forces, and the Treasury mandarins observed that the Corporation was wasting money on buying 'worthless rookeries' in the city centre instead of building on the relatively clear site at Fairbrothers' Field, which had been used for market gardening after the local textile industries disappeared.

In May 1918 Lord French replaced Lord Wimborne as Lord Lieutenant, while Edward Shortt took over from Henry Duke for a brief eight-month stint as chief secretary. Because of the uproar it provoked, moves to introduce conscription to Ireland were abandoned and, by late June, the Castle was again attempting to deflect criticism by stressing important social issues such as urban housing. Although the Irish Parliamentary Party was in terminal decline, it attempted to fight Ireland's corner on the issue of post-war housing in the House of Commons, where its leader was Joseph Devlin, the MP for West Belfast. He pointed out that if MPs abstained from attending parliament, as Sinn Féin was suggesting, Ireland was unlikely to get any further subsidies for housing and that the Ulster Unionists would make up the largest Irish party in Westminster.

After the 1918 ceasefire, fears that the return of five million trained soldiers from the trenches of Europe could result in a Bolshevik-style revolt found the British government promoting the 'Homes Fit for Heroes to Live in' campaign. Centralised state subsidies were available to local authorities in both Britain and Ireland and a government grant in the form of a fixed percentage of the annual charge for principal and interest would allow for subsidised rents and prevent local authorities from going into serious debt.

In December 1918 came the first post-war election, with David Lloyd George of the Liberal Party elected prime minister of a coalition government. Sinn Féin swept away the remnants of the Irish Parliamentary Party when winning 73 of the 105 Irish seats in the House of Commons and then, as promised before the election, refusing to take up its quota of seats. In January 1919 the elected Sinn Féin deputies met at Dublin's Mansion House and declared themselves the Government of Ireland, or Dáil Éireann. William Cosgrave, who had chaired Dublin Corporation's Housing Committee, became the unofficial Minister for Local Government.

With the new Dáil quickly outlawed, the Local Government Board's Housing Committee continued to direct overall policy and the Housing (Ireland) Act 1919 marked a major development. As well as subsidies from the Treasury for local authorities building houses, a lesser grant was on offer to public utility societies and housing trusts, while private tenants could buy their houses with low-interest loans. Compensation in compulsory orders cases was reduced, simplifying the procedure for acquiring sites. With the Local Government Board putting Peter Cowan in charge of a new Housing Department, three large projects were underway by early 1920, partly financed by British grants. However, when it became clear that most local authorities backed the unofficial Dáil, the Local Government Board stopped all financial assistance.

In the years following the end of the war, the lack of the skilled architects and draughtsmen needed to design the proposed housing schemes became a problem. Charles McCarthy caused controversy when he suggested that the Corporation enlist six architects to prepare plans and supervise eight proposed schemes without advertising the roles through an open competition. As an alternative, Horace O'Rourke suggested that he be put in charge of the proposed schemes, acting either as architect to the Housing Committee or as a director of housing. Nothing came of his suggestion and outside architects were taken on in 1920. Later schemes relied solely on the Housing Department's own team, promoting conformity in design and layout plans. McCarthy would resign in 1921, citing ill health as the reason; O'Rourke succeeded him. The position was not advertised.

In the local elections of 1920, when proportional representation was used for the first time, Sinn Féin won 560 seats in local councils, while Labour, with 394 seats emerged as the second-biggest party. It meant that loans and subsidies from London would now be going to councils dominated by labour activists and die-hard separatists. Yet under draft plans for Home Rule, which allowed limited devolution to the two Irish administrations in Dublin and Belfast, the British Cabinet agreed to continue financing Irish state housing after the transfer of power. A sum of £2 million for seven years was proposed; the Treasury baulked and cut that number by half.

In April 1920 Hamar Greenwood was appointed chief secretary along with a new breed of progressive officials whose brief was to shake up Dublin Castle's sluggish administration. Sir John Anderson, joint under-secretary, would head a newly-created Irish Treasury. Progress was hindered by open hostility between Sinn Féin and the Castle administration after the Cabinet decided that the local council should pay for any damage to a city's property during the ongoing War of Independence.

For most of the Corporation staff, life continued as usual. Following work on the Spitalfields scheme, cottages were built at St James's Walk and then at Ceannt Fort before attention finally turned to the Fairbrothers' Fields site. Galloping inflation had seen the price of materials soaring. Building materials cost up to five times more than before the war, and labourers' wages, which accounted for almost half the price of building a house, had more than doubled. Brick earth was scarce in Ireland and the best carpenters and joiners were employed in the shipyards. A house built for £900 in 1914 now cost £3,500 to complete.

At Fairbrothers' Fields, Dublin Corporation, hoping to cut costs, decided to use direct labour and make use of the guild system. At Ellenfield, off the Swords Road at Whitehall, direct labour through a site manager was used, although this saved little in expenditure since the Corporation workers were well paid.

In June 1920 the Dáil, though still illegal, ordered local councils to sever their connection to the Local Government Board; municipal housing initiatives funded by an alien government could not be supported. By August of that year the Corporation was in danger of bankruptcy, owing £160,000 to the contractors for the McCaffrey Estate and St James's Walk schemes alone. To reduce its deficit, it sold stock to the Bank of Ireland and suspended all further housing work.

By April 1921, some 372 local authorities had either refused to recognise the Local Government Board or were ambivalent. The truce in the War of Independence came in mid-July, followed by the controversial Anglo-Irish Treaty creating the Irish Free State, which was signed in December 1921. The Local Government Board was shut down, with only 300 of the planned 50,000 dwellings in Ireland completed.

In 1922 Abercrombie's 1914 plan for remodelling Dublin was finally published. Abercrombie himself admitted that the original scheme, as a competition entry, tended towards the spectacular at the expense of the practical, ignoring the necessities of ordinary life: easy access to work for the adults and to schools and play areas for children. Its attitude to tenement housing, regarding tenements as 'a sort of clearing house during the immense operation of rehousing' could at best be described as ambiguous. Few foresaw the impact that the arrival of private transport would have on city planning; Geddes had regarded the obsession with motor cars as 'a temporary intoxication' and 'a malady of youth'.

4

The 'Million Pound Scheme'

Before April 1922 the Corporation had erected 2,243 dwellings, over half as cottages, and acquired a further 1,507 dwellings, 80 per cent of them cottages. An estimated 17,593 houses were still needed in the Corporation area and a further 2,124 in neighbouring districts. After independence, the Irish Free State was in charge of providing housing for its citizens, yet the Land Act of 1923 made no mention of town tenants. Flats made up only 8 per cent of dwellings between 1922 and 1932 when the idea of tenants purchasing their properties over a number of years through a mortgage took hold. Those who could not afford a mortgage were ignored and, although the Town Tenants' League met Michael Collins and Arthur Griffith to highlight unfair evictions, exorbitant rents and other injustices, the Free State's ideology remained deeply anti-urban and socially conservative. The elite of independent Ireland, drawn mainly from the property-owning bourgeoisie, were as reluctant to interfere with the property rights of landlords as had been their predecessors.

Still, a new approach was obviously required and, after the transfer of power in 1922, William Cosgrave had launched the 'Million Pound Scheme' under which municipalities would build 2,150 new urban houses at an average cost of £750 and with an average rent of 10s 6d. To avail of the scheme, councils would raise £125,000 by a charge of a penny in the pound on rates and borrow £375,000 on the open market. The Free State would match that sum of £500,000, so bringing it up to a million. As a result 2,000 houses were built by twenty local authorities between 1922 and 1924, mainly in Dublin and surrounding areas.

Although Cosgrave used the 'Million Pound Scheme' while campaigning before the 1923 general election, his government abandoned any pretence at trying to solve the housing problem after it was elected. Under the Housing Act of 1924 it offered a subsidy to private builders, who proved more interested in building for the better-off. When in 1924 Captain William Redmond introduced bills in the Dáil to give town tenants the three Fs – fair rent, free sale and fixity of tenure – he was not successful. Landlords had already been hit by the Rent Restrictions Act of 1915 which, when it was fully implemented in 1923, helped convert the better-off Irish into owner-occupiers and the less affluent into local-authority tenants. Home owners were given remission from paying rates for several years after they bought a house. Further legislation in 1929 would make granting of rates remission compulsory, so depriving local authorities of much-needed funding and undermining their ability to borrow.

The Free State government, headed by Cosgrave, adopted British policies with slight adjustments and absorbed the existing Dublin Castle administration into its burgeoning civil service. Among the new appointees was Peter Cowan of the Local Government Board, although in February 1923 his appointment was terminated after just ten months, despite his widely acknowledged ability and dedication.

By 1924 public spending was cut by over 40 per cent to balance the budget. From 1922 to 1932, fewer than 10,000 subsidised dwellings were built by local authorities, compared to 16,500 by private builders. Architects, and indeed builders, were involved in both private and public schemes; the Vernon estate in Clontarf, for instance, saw private building on Corporation land, which was a new venture. Building, both public and private, provided jobs, with the needs of former National Army soldiers in particular promoted. Many builders were also politicians or had the ear of a politician; those desperately seeking a roof over their head had little or no influence.

From 1924 to 1930 Dublin Corporation was dissolved as part of the Cosgrave government's 'centralising' policy, which meant that elected councils in most cities were disbanded. Cosgrave, as a former Dublin city councillor, was well aware of how a city council could be subverted by factions and, at the time, Dublin Corporation was dominated by rebel anti-Treaty councillors. It was replaced by three biddable commissioners with impeccable records in public service: Dr William Dwyer and Seamus Ó Murchadha came from the Dublin Union, while Patrick Hernon, a Galway-born inspector with the Department of Local Government from 1921 to 1923, was commissioner of Cork Poor Law Union at the time of his appointment. He would later become city manager. Top priority for the trio was cutting costs and, while they certainly did some good work, initiative was stifled and local concerns ignored.

Construction had resumed at the Fairbrothers' Fields site in 1922 using a short-term Corporation loan, and the estate, following garden-suburb design principles, was eventually completed in 1927 under the 'Million Pound Scheme'. The estate, reduced from 22 to 16 acres, provided 334 five-roomed cottages, with parlours and the toilet on the first floor, at a cost of around £955 each, plus eighty-two four-roomed houses, mostly built in the final phase, costing £677 each. Designs were influenced both by Unwin and the Liverpool School of Architecture's neoclassical style, with setbacks and culs-de-sac as well as other neoclassical references. The revised scheme featured in the *Architect* periodical; it was the first Irish housing project to receive such an accolade.

Thanks largely to the input of the Dublin Building Trades Guild, which had received a number of contracts from the Corporation between 1921 and 1924, the quality of the houses was exceptional, but because guild labour proved more expensive than anticipated, the guild was not called upon again after the parsimonious city commissioners took responsibility for the city's housing projects.

Fairbrothers' Fields was the Corporation's first venture into tenant purchase, with new houses sold off to tenants by charging them a weekly 'payback' system instead of rent. Over the next decade or so, all the council's inter-war suburban cottages were sold to tenants, making up a total of 4,248 dwellings, or about a quarter of Dublin Corporation's housing stock. Aimed at the better-off working-classes, the Fairbrothers' Fields and the McCaffrey schemes did little to alleviate the situation of the poorest working-class families.

Even more ambitious than Fairbrothers' Fields was a return to the Marino garden-suburb plan. When the Corporation included the Marino estate in the 'Million Pound Scheme', the site was enlarged to 126 acres and the design handed over to Frederick G. Hicks, an English-born Arts and Crafts architect who had lived and worked in Dublin since 1890. The estate of 1,262 houses was built on the site of a planned formal garden for Marino House, with the Hicks design centred on two circular greens from which roads to four other circles radiated. The two-storey houses, mostly five-roomed with front and rear gardens, came in a variety of designs and included terraces with plain pebble-dash exteriors for the less affluent. A big influence was the Unwin-designed Roehampton garden suburb estate in London, which Corporation officials visited in 1923. Unusually for the time, the houses were built in concrete rather than brick, and a German firm specialising in concrete-building techniques was hired along with local firms H. & J. Martin and G. & T. Crampton. The Marino garden suburb was the Corporation's most successful and best-designed scheme with its narrow roads and open green spaces.

Despite a three-month workers' dispute in 1924, the scheme was completed in 1927. Houses were sold to tenant purchasers at prices of between £400 and £440; with weekly payments coming out at between 15s to 16s 1d depending on the house, it was certainly not aimed at the urban poor.

Work on Donnelly's Orchard, a scheme of eighty-four tenant-purchase brick-faced cottages at Clonliffe Road, began in October 1923, with H. & J. Martin the contractors. As in Marino, most of the brick-faced houses had five rooms. In the mid-1920s came a return to smaller houses, largely because of the rising cost of materials, with allegations of price-fixing among suppliers rife. Labour was also proving more expensive, especially after the working week was reduced from fifty to forty-four hours.

Drumcondra, built in 1928, was less varied in design than Marino, although the site, sloping down to the Tolka river at Griffith Park, added interest. The scheme consisted of 211 three-roomed, 144 four-roomed and 180 five-roomed houses built in pairs, threes, fours and fives, some in culs-de-sac and with attractive corner houses. As in Marino, the Corporation made use of the 'reserved order' concept by which part of a development site was zoned for private houses. As well as improving the look of an area, these private schemes created a better social mix and helped raise the rates income from a development.

With state funds directed to tenant-purchase garden-suburb schemes, only a few small blocks of municipal flats were built during the 1920s. An exception to garden-suburb dominance was the Boyne Street project, built alongside stables used by coal-carrying dray horses behind Westland Row Station from 1922 to 1923, which featured an innovative 'maisonette' plan designed by George L. O'Connor. At the front of each three-storey block were two hall doors to the ground-floor lettings, while at the back were four hall doors leading to self-contained cottages. Each of the seventy-eight dwellings had a living room, two bedrooms, a kitchen, a scullery and a water closet. The ground and first floors were faced with Irish red brick from Courtown; the top floor was built of County Dublin brickwork and a cement pebble-dash exterior. Although its unusual design provoked a storm of protest, the scheme has weathered well.

Less successful was a flat-based scheme at the former Richmond Barracks in Inchicore: Abercrombie had suggested requisitioning former barracks for housing in his 1914 plan. Renamed Keogh Barracks, the complex was leased to Dublin Corporation from October 1924 for ninety-eight years. By 1927, 202 flats, as well as twenty-four temporary three-roomed dwellings in the 13-acre field east of the square, were completed. There were also shops, a milk depot in the former officers' mess, and a 36-acre market garden. In total, the scheme housed some 248 families in the flats, with a further 218 families in houses. Each three-storey 'hall' housed six families, two on each floor. Although the flats had their own small kitchen and toilet, a generous living room with an open fire, and two or three bedrooms, the utilitarian origins of the scheme could not be disguised. Called Keogh Square, the scheme degenerated into one of Dublin's most notorious slums. It was demolished in 1969 when it was replaced by the equally problematic St Michael's Estate, itself demolished in 2013.

In September 1925 a 99-year lease was taken out on the former Linenhall Barracks on Lurgan Street where it was planned initially to construct seventy temporary dwellings; eventually, the Linenhall Public Utility Society came up with a plan for sixty-three houses. Other barracks used for housing were Marshalsea Barracks, with fifty-three flats completed in 1931, and Beggars Bush, with forty-four flats available from 1933.

In 1925 the Minister for Local Government, Seán T. O'Kelly, issued the first publication on native housing and house design as prescribed by the government. It would grow to five volumes of house types and specifications, with London County Council schemes a major influence and the more innovative approaches used by other major European cities largely ignored. Crumlin was the first of many schemes built according to these standards, which would remain in place for decades.

A plan for building a block of forty flats at Crabbe Lane off Upper Mercer Street, a site first inspected by Charles McCarthy in 1914, was revived in 1926 and saw Herbert Simms making his first appearance in the story of Dublin's social housing. By this time employed by the city architect's office on a contract, Simms was sent to London, Liverpool and Manchester to inspect the latest in flat-block design, with his expenses for the trip amounting to £18 17s 3d. He would have noted that designs in Britain had become more ambitious, especially in the matter of access to the flats, with a move away from expensive multi-stairwells serving two to four flats, to one stairwell and access along an exterior gallery or deck. All flats had private toilets, and the schemes included coal stores and pram sheds.

Block schemes were not entirely unfamiliar to Dubliners, thanks to the DADC flats from the 1870s at

Buckingham and Dominick streets and the Corporation's own blocks at Benburb Street, Bow Lane, Foley Street and Townsend Street, as well as the mix of flats and cottages at Ormond Market. Arguably setting the standard was the imposing Iveagh Trust scheme at Bull Alley, which was built from 1899 to 1906. The five-storey blocks featured a mansard roof faced in red brick.

Despite Simms' researches into urban flat building, the Dublin commissioners continued their policy of low-density garden-suburb tenant-purchase schemes aimed at middle-income workers. Private developers were following their lead and, from the mid-1920s, shoddily-built ribbons of private suburban housing were attracting criticism. The city's administration had only limited control over development. When a developer defied both the city architect's advice and city by-laws, there was nothing the city's commissioners could – or would – do.

For the first time in fifteen years, a census was held in 1926. It found that over a third of all Dublin working-class families were still living in tenements, many of them in a single room with no cleaning, cooking or toilet facilities. The Corporation was criticised for building barrack-like flats, which bred discontent and were ripe for 'Communist' infiltration. From 1926 to 1936, 21,262 families had moved into the greater Dublin area which, after 1930, included Rathmines, Rathgar and Pembroke.

In early Corporation schemes, most dwellings had three rooms, although at Foley Street, a number of one-room apartments were included in the plans. None of those built before 1923 had more than four rooms. After the 1922 Housing Committee recommended a better class of dwelling, a minimum three bedrooms was suggested; one for the boys, one for the girls and one for the parents. A 'parlour' was considered essential for household morale, if nothing else, and so a five-room dwelling was considered the most appropriate for the average family. For aesthetic reasons, the semi-detached house was rejected in favour of terraces of four to six buildings.

After 1928, with costs increasing, the size of houses began to shrink. Despite the large size of the average Irish family, the final tenant-purchase schemes of 1930–31 favoured four rooms rather than five. Even after the serious attempts to remove the slums from 1932 to 1937, two-thirds of dwellings had three rooms and a quarter had four rooms. No further five-roomed dwellings were built by the Corporation until 1958.

Developments sanctioned by the city commissioners towards the end of the 1920s included the Butterly estate, off Home Farm Road at the back of St Patrick's College, and Donnycarney, developed from 1929 to 1931 to the south of Collins Avenue. From 1930, the city commissioners built thirty-two houses from St Declan's Terrace to Turlough Parade on Griffith Avenue, with the houses costing £715 each.

Ireland's first comprehensive town-planning bill was passed in May 1929, although it did not come into force until 1934. Under its provisions, every local authority was ordered to prepare a civic study of the lands, water and buildings in its area within three years, taking into consideration social conditions and communications.

In December 1930 a slimmed-down Dublin Corporation was reinstated, with the number of councillors reduced from eighty-four to thirty-five. Alfie Byrne was named Lord Mayor and would serve for nine consecutive years. Gerald Sherlock, then the town clerk, was appointed manager of an enlarged city, which now included the Pembroke and Rathmines townships. Dún Laoghaire would remain independent with the Dublin commissioner Patrick Hernon appointed borough manager. He would return to Dublin as city manager in 1937 after Sherlock retired.

Not until the 1931 Housing (Miscellaneous Provisions) Act did the focus of housing policy return to slum clearance. A view that state intervention was necessary to manage the increasingly overcrowded cities of Europe had taken a firm hold and the 1931 act made the process of acquiring sites by compulsory order less costly, with compensation based only on the value of the site, minus the cost of clearing it, and local authorities freed from the burden of paying all the annual charges on loans taken out to fund public housing.

In 1931 the city architect Horace O'Rourke was ordered to construct a model of a tenement flat with the aid of Herbert Simms. The overall design adapted

European modernism with access off open balconies facing internal courtyards and an attempt to build in sympathy with the surrounding streets. The model flat, on view at the Mansion House in late September 1931, was equipped with hot water, electric lighting and gas for cooking and consisted of three rooms, a toilet and a scullery (with bath). Among those photographed viewing the model were several officials from the Department of Local Government and local councillors, as well as O'Rourke and Simms.

The plan was to erect a block of such flats at St Mary's Lane, where each flat would cost about £380 to build after the site was acquired and cleared. The total 'all-in' cost of each dwelling was about £550, largely because of the cost of acquiring and clearing sites in the slum areas in the city centre. If rented at 7s a week, well beyond the means of the average unskilled labourer, a three-roomed flat in the city would need a subsidy of £25 a year.

In the general election held on 16 February 1932, Fianna Fáil, with the support of the Labour Party, came to power. So ended nine years of conservative Cumann na nGaedheal rule. Now it was the turn of Éamon de Valera, promising a form of economic nationalism which would include increased public spending on housing.

5

Herbert Simms:
a man with a mission

Herbert George Simms was born in London on 30 November 1898. His father, George William Simms, a former shepherd from Fawley, Buckinghamshire, was by then working as a train driver; his mother was Nellie Worster of Hemel Hempstead. He was the eldest of six children from his father's second marriage; five sons and a daughter. Simms' father already had two sons and two daughters from his first marriage. His wife Mahala had died in 1896, aged thirty-nine.

At the time of Herbert's birth, the family, including the half-siblings, lived at Prince of Wales Road in Kentish Town. The children attended the local Haverstock Industrial and Commercial School. In 1911 the growing family moved to 33 Victoria Road, off Kilburn High Road.

During the First World War, Simms served in the Royal Field Artillery and was possibly under the minimum age of eighteen when he joined up. The Royal Field Artillery, responsible for medium-calibre guns and howitzers deployed close to the front line, was the largest arm of the artillery. When he was demobbed in 1919 at the age of twenty, Simms was awarded an ex-serviceman's scholarship of £150, which enabled him to study architecture at Liverpool University for three years. Why he chose such a career is unknown. Architecture as a profession was still in its infancy; the University College of Liverpool, which was the forerunner of Liverpool University, had set up its degree course in architecture in 1894 when Frederick Moore Simpson was appointed professor. In 1902 Liverpool became the first university School of Architecture in Britain to offer accredited degrees in architecture. The charismatic Charles Reilly, who succeeded Simpson as professor of the faculty in 1904, was a neoclassicist who believed that Beaux-Arts design was the only way out of what he perceived as Arts and Crafts amateurism. Students of the college became renowned for their solid grasp of traditional good design and practice.

Simms started his course in September 1919 and received the Certificate in Architecture in 1921, two years after beginning his studies. He passed the third and fourth years of the diploma course in June 1921 and June 1922, at which point he was forced to give up his studies for financial reasons. He was a talented student and, in the summer term of 1922, was permitted to study for the Certificate in Civic Design in lieu of practical work because of his previous office experience and the high standard he had achieved. In June 1923 he was elected an associate of the Royal Institute of British Architects (RIBA), having sat the Special War Exam; he was proposed by Charles Reilly, John Murray and Sir Henry Tanner.

Soon after, Simms came to Dublin to take up a job with Aubrey Vincent O'Rourke, a brother of the Dublin city architect Horace Tennyson O'Rourke, who had started his own architectural practice at Prudential Chambers, College Green, in 1914. O'Rourke, who would die in 1928 at the early age of forty-three, was developing a busy commercial practice.

By February 1925 Simms, along with J.B. McMahon, had joined Dublin Corporation as a temporary architect with a salary of eight guineas a week. Both their contracts, initially for six months, were later extended until at least December 1927. It was during this period that Simms was sent on the tour of London, Liverpool and Manchester to investigate the latest trends in flat-building for the working classes. With the Corporation chronically understaffed, the work was demanding and yet Simms and others were still only engaged on temporary contracts. In 1928 he was awarded a Diploma in Town Planning from the RIBA and became an associate member of the Town Planning Institute.

A few months later Simms left the Corporation to work briefly as a town planner in the Punjab, India. Later references to a nervous breakdown early in his career may refer to this period since he only spent about six months in India. At the time, prominent British architects, including Sir Edwin Lutyens and Sir Herbert Baker, were working on major building projects for the British Raj. Basil Martin Sullivan, the superintending architect and Town Planner to the Punjab, was responsible for a number of significant buildings in the neoclassical style as well as a 'model town' scheme based on garden-city principles, in Lahore. A decade earlier, Patrick Geddes had spent some time in India, becoming professor of sociology and civics at Bombay University between 1919 and 1925 and producing town-planning reports on a number of cities, including Lahore.

Like Geddes, Simms would embrace a strongly ethical approach to town planning and public housing. By June 1929 he was back in Ireland and was finally given a permanent position. Along with the Scotsman Robert Sorley Lawrie, he was appointed an assistant architect to the Dublin City Commissioners at a starting salary of £280, which would rise by £15 increments to £400.

Three months later, on 30 September 1929, Simms, with his future prospects secure, married Eileen Florence Clarke of 76 Carysfort Avenue, Blackrock, at the Church of St John the Baptist in Blackrock. Eileen, born in 1908, was the daughter of Garda Superintendent Thomas

Clarke and his wife Agnes (*née* Grogan) of Mount Merrion. Witnesses to the wedding were Robert Lawrie and Violet Clarke. At the time of his marriage, Simms, described as a civil servant, was living at 111 North Circular Road.

When in late 1930 a slimmed-down Dublin Corporation was reinstated, it reverted to the view that it should provide housing for those unable to pay for a deposit on a house. Mount Pleasant and Hollyfields were two flat schemes begun by the Rathmines Urban District Council and completed by the Corporation in June 1931, with each flat costing £346. At a rent of 2s 6d per room, the loss on each dwelling was £770 a year. Rent strikes were among the many problems facing the Corporation's Housing Department.

In October 1931 Simms prepared a memorandum on Vienna's public housing schemes, describing how the Austrian city had spent £750,000 a year on housing over the previous eight years, raising the necessary funding through a housing tax on income. In Vienna, housing for all was considered a basic human right, and it expected to have 62,000 meticulously-designed dwellings completed by 1932. Simms concluded that while they could take inspiration from the Viennese schemes, the city's customs and economic conditions were very different to those of Dublin. In 1919, after the collapse of the Austro-Hungarian Empire, the Social Democratic Party had become the dominant party in

the city's legislature, initiating a radical reformist programme of municipal socialism – mass housebuilding,
public education and healthcare.

When the newly-created post of housing architect
for Dublin city was advertised, with specific responsibility for the design and erection of new dwellings as
distinct from administration and maintenance, Simms
was offered the job, which he took up in January 1932
– just a few weeks before Fianna Fáil, led by Éamon de
Valera, moved into government. With the country's new
leaders aiming to meet all housing needs in ten years, the
top priority of urban authorities became slum clearance.
A major obstacle to their plans was the exorbitant cost of
acquiring and clearing the slum sites, often controlled by
a bewildering hierarchy of landlords, all seeking financial
compensation. To house the poorest of the poor, a basic
rent of 2s a week for a flat or 2s 6d per room in a cottage, far below the average rent paid for privately-owned
accommodation, was proposed. At the time, family
income for a quarter of the city's workers ranged from
5s to 20s and even a low rent was a heavy burden. The
trade unionist William O'Brien had argued that rent in
public housing should amount to no more than 10 per
cent of wages.

An innovative proposal to establish a housing board
with the authority to requisition land compulsorily
emerged in 1932; such a board could also make, sell or
buy building materials, and establish co-operatives for

this purpose. When eventually established, the board proved much weaker than hoped for, often enlisting the assistance of Fianna Fáil deputies to put pressure on sluggish local authorities. Under the Housing (Financial and Miscellaneous Provisions) Act of 1932, the state contribution to slum clearance equalled two-thirds of the annual loan charges, which was effectively double the previous terms. Design standards improved, helped by a fall in the cost of housebuilding – a 500-square-foot house now cost £350 to build.

For a brief period after the election, the Labour Party held the balance of power and it pressurised the government into raising income tax to pay for increased investment in housing and other social issues. At the time there were over 11,000 applications for public housing. Appointed Minister for Local Government and Public Health was Seán T. O'Kelly, whose younger brother Michael was an architect working with Horace O'Rourke's department in the Corporation.

At the housing architect's office at 3 Parliament Street, Simms supervised a large and ever-changing staff of assistant architects, draughtsmen, quantity surveyors and clerical assistants. In 1933, a year after the office was established, all three of the assistant architects were First World War veterans. Dublin native John Edward Burke had served in a variety of roles, most notably as an observation officer in the balloon section of the Royal Flying Corps. Raymond Croisdale Stevenson, an Englishman who had served as a private in a non-combatant corps, had previously worked with Simms in the city architect's office and was a talented draughtsman and artist. Richard David Graham, from Belfast, had moved to Dublin in 1931 to take up the post of assistant architect to the Irish Sailors' and Soldiers' Land Trust. He joined the Housing Architect's Department of Dublin Corporation in September 1932 and died in July 1933 aged forty-three, just a month before his appointment was to be extended.

There were also four draughtsmen, most notably Cecil Francis Higginbotham who, in 1936, became assistant architect to Dún Laoghaire Borough Council. In 1946 he returned to Dublin Corporation as senior building surveyor, rising in 1948 to the position of senior building surveyor and surveyor for places of public resort, a position previously held by his father until 1943. Thomas Carberry, a member of a well-known family of builders based in Athy and Carlow, emerged from University College Dublin with a B Arch degree in 1929, spending only a brief time with the Housing Architect's Department, while M. O'Kelly and A.W. Browett were the other two draughtsmen.

John O'Brien was the quantity surveyor, while a temporary employee in his section was the veteran architect Denis Joseph Hickie, who had worked with the DADC as an assistant to architect Charles Ashworth from 1896, later becoming the company's chief engineer. In 1922 he had transferred to the Department of Local

Government, where he worked on housing schemes in Dublin and surrounding counties. Rounding out the staff roster were Misses D.E. O'Rourke (who was possibly O'Rourke's daughter Ethel), and R. Wills, who worked as temporary 'improvers'.

Student architects in the department were Dermod O'Rourke and Emmet Humphreys. Soon after graduating from UCD in 1934, O'Rourke, a son of Horace, joined the architectural staff of the Office of Public Works (OPW). Humphreys, a staunch republican whose education was interrupted by a number of jail sentences, had also graduated from UCD in 1934. In 1947 he was appointed chief architect in the Department of Local Government. Superintendent of the Housing Department was P.J. Dillon, with Leo Lawlor as his assistant. Medical officer of health for County Dublin was Dr John Austin Harbison.

At some time before 1937 Charles McNamara, who had initially worked in the city architect's office, moved to the housing architect's office and later became Simms' assistant, while Ernest Taylor became chief quantity surveyor.

The work was complex. After a site was judged suitable for building, sketch plans to explain the general layout and elevations of the scheme were prepared. Once these were approved, work began on drawings and specifications, giving all the important dimensions and indicating the construction and finish of the buildings. Under Simms' direction, the drawings were typically prepared by the assistant architects, helped by two draughtsmen. From the drawings, the quantity surveyors assessed the likely cost of the job before tenders were invited. They also prepared monthly progress charts and kept a check on contractors' claims for payments. Securing qualified assistant quantity surveyors proved difficult.

Simms himself was a prodigious worker, instigating the compulsory orders for all the schemes, signing off the overall design of every building and working closely with the Corporation's quantity surveyors on hiring contractors and procuring materials. He attended building inquiries and dealt with the demands of politicians, churchmen, pressure groups and trade unions. On the flat-block schemes, he would continue to organise extra features, such as playgrounds, pram sheds and spaces for laundry, long after residents had moved in.

When it came to the housing schemes on the fringes of the city, fitting in churches, schools, shops and parks, as well as street lighting and drainage, proved an exhausting and thankless task, with many competing interests to juggle. As Simms himself put it, '… you cannot rehouse a population of 15,000 people, as in the Crumlin scheme, without providing for the other necessities and amenities of life'. He didn't always get his way. When the first residents moved into Crumlin, the only civic amenity was a 900-seat Catholic church. Two years after they first arrived, the children of the area were still travelling back to their old schools in the city and, with the bus service both erratic and pricey, truancy was rampant.

In May 1932 Simms told the annual meeting of the Irish Free State District of the Municipal and County Engineers in Dawson Street, Dublin that the absence of a town plan militated against the solution of one of Dublin's greatest problems – the abolition of the slums.

Without a town plan, he said, the 'town beautiful' of the future would never materialise. Planning was needed so that zones for industry, housing and amenities were organised in relation to the town as a whole. Current policy was to clear and develop small isolated sites.

Another difficulty was providing alternative accommodation for dispossessed tenants. Workers needed to live near their jobs; a fact overlooked when slum-dwellers were given houses miles away from the city docks and other places employing casual labour. In the previous ten years Dublin Corporation had built approximately 4,500 dwellings, of which the majority were four- and five-roomed houses; only 126 were flats. Rents ranged from 13s to 17s a week for the four- and five-roomed houses and from 5s to 10s for the remainder. These rents did not cover the cost of building and maintaining those dwellings. Financial assistance from the government and some contributions from the city rates helped to reduce the annual deficit. It was hoped, Simms said, to provide a flat consisting of living room, bedroom, scullery, toilet, coal bunker and hall for a weekly rent of 5s.

In 1933 the pace of building accelerated. Slum areas already cleared included Mary's Lane, Mercer Street, Cook Street, Hanover Street, Mountrath Street and Chancery Place. In the financial year ending 31 March 1933, 251 dwellings were completed. By 31 March 1934 an additional 910 had been built. Among them were the forty-four flats, thirty-one of them three-roomed and thirteen of them two-roomed, at the Beggars Bush barracks off Shelbourne Road in Ballsbridge.

At a February 1933 conference held in the Mansion House to consider the housing question, with both Simms and the city manager, Gerald Sherlock, attending, the Lord Mayor of Dublin, Alfie Byrne, announced that in the previous fourteen months some 1,600 families had been housed, while 3,000 more houses, extending over seven miles of roadway, were under construction in the Crumlin area. A further conference was held a fortnight later.

Simms was called to speak at a public sitting of the Free State Prices Commission held in Dublin that May, where he gave evidence on the cost of materials and appliances used in constructing houses. In his opinion there was a definite shortage of housing materials, while a shortage of skilled labour often increased the costs of building because of the delay in completing the houses. When asked whether there was price-fixing among builders' providers, Simms diplomatically replied that since builders' providers were all quoting the same prices for contracts, the element of competition had been reduced. Buying direct was not an option – if builders' providers found out, they could boycott contractors and hold up work.

In a £300 house, £98-worth of the materials came from local companies. Simms' department aimed to use Irish materials when possible and in the previous five years, the proportion of Irish materials used had doubled. With the present increase in building, the cost of building materials should have decreased with manufacturers accepting a lower profit, he pointed out. The reverse had happened and the prices of sand and gravel had increased, although a Sand and Gravel Merchants' Association was formed to control prices, prevent cut-throat competition and regularise wages paid to quarry labour.

On 26 July 1933 the British Medical Association held its annual conference in Dublin, with Simms speaking on public housing at a meeting held in Trinity College. Although ideally a family home should contain five rooms, it was absolutely impossible to provide such a house at a rent the poorest could pay, he said. In the suburbs, the weekly rent for a house with a living room, two bedrooms and a scullery, was 7s 6d.

Since the Corporation had acquired sites such as Cook Street and Mary's Lane in earlier years, 1933 and 1934 were boom years for housing development. During the financial year ending 31 March 1934 approximately 1,000 dwellings were almost complete, with a further

2,300 dwellings put out to contract. The pace would slow when the authorities were forced to find new sites, with the procedure for clearing areas both time-consuming and frustrating and often involving a public inquiry. For example, although plans for the Hanover Street development were drawn up in 1931, building was still going on in 1937. Existing tenants had to be housed elsewhere, a process inelegantly called 'decanting', and not all were happy to take the long hike to the suburbs. For Mary's Lane, tenants were rehoused locally; for Cook Street, the residents were sent to Beggsboro in Cabra.

After Raymond Unwin gave a lecture called 'Planning Towns for Modern Life' at the Mansion House in October 1933, Lord Mayor Alfie Byrne pointed out that there were 11,300 applications for the meagre 400 cottages the Corporation had at its disposal.

Towards the end of November, Simms and some of his staff joined Thomas Kelly and a group from the Corporation's Housing Committee to inspect the derelict areas of James's Street, Basin Street, Irwin Street, Marrowbone Lane, Robert Street, Bow's Lane, Ardee Street, Newmarket and Cook Street, described by Kelly as 'one of the most deplorable abominations of the housing problem'.

Before the end of that year, the Housing Committee approved compulsory orders under the North City Clearance Scheme for stretches of Sean McDermott Street from the Gloucester Diamond to Gloucester

Lane and, on Railway Street from Corporation Street to Beaver Street, as well as Purdon Street, the east side of Corporation Street, and Gloucester Place Lower. Simms had already prepared a layout for the erection of 272 dwellings, while plans were underway for a derelict site in North Cumberland Street and for about a hundred dwellings on the grounds attached to Aldborough House.

One of Simms' first projects after returning to Dublin from India was Mercer House in the Crabbe Lane area off Upper Mercer Street and behind the Royal College of Surgeons. Work on Mercer House, a four-storey block designed by Horace O'Rourke, had begun in 1929, with H. & J. Martin the contractors. Phase 2, designed by Simms and perhaps Robert Lawrie, began after the purchase of adjoining lands in 1932 and was completed in 1934, providing 104 flats. The scheme was extended in 1937. After Mercer House came Simms' first individual effort: St Michan's House in the notorious slum area of Greek Street, located behind the Bridewell and close to the Four Courts. When the complex of 120 flats was completed in 1934, it was considered as good a public housing building as anything in Berlin, Moscow or Vienna.

Simms' next completed scheme, built between 1934 and 1935 in just eight months, was the Amsterdam-influenced Chancery House in Charles Street, not far from St Michan's House. Although small – providing only twenty-seven flats – the scheme, including a compact garden reached through an elegant arched entrance, was widely admired. In 1935 Simms had attended the fourteenth International Housing and Town Planning Congress in London, revisiting schemes in London and elsewhere and keeping up to date with the latest trends in architecture. He later told the 1939 Housing Inquiry that he firmly believed the homes he was constructing would outlast the slum dwellings they were replacing. To him, 'flats should last at least 200 years ... providing they were properly maintained'.

One of Simms' early jobs was providing shelters along Clontarf promenade, where work had begun in 1911 when a concrete sea wall 45.7 metres from the existing sea wall at the Fairview end of Clontarf was con-structed. The space between was a dump, filled with the city's waste until the 1920s. With the Clontarf baths in existence since 1881 and the Bull Wall created between 1819 and 1825 to tackle silting in Dublin Bay, Clontarf was a popular bathing site on the north side of the city.

Shelters were built from the 1930s, with the seven modernist examples designed by Simms appearing in 1934. Some were for bathing and others for seating. The first two were built of pre-cast, reinforced concrete with an unpainted finish, although supposed to be painted in cream and black, with a concrete bench inside. Simms' original plan for at least one enclosed kiosk with a coun-ter and café seating was never realised; the two shelters with seats are adaptations of that design. The other five shelters are designed for bathers, with three for men and two for women. These were built in pre-cast concrete painted yellow with hand-painted signage, consisting of a long wall parallel to the promenade. Inside is a bench with a central portal opening and a round-edged, square canopy supported on rounded columns. Only in 1958 was the scheme finally completed.

In 1934 the newly-established Town Planning Committee of the Corporation was calling for increased state aid for housing. Since the Corporation's debt stood at over £6 million, and Dublin rates were already not only the highest in Ireland but also higher than in any British city, the 1934 housing programme would require raising almost £2.8 million in the next two years. Not helping was the Small Dwellings Acquisition Act, under which the Corporation was obliged to provide grants to prospective house-buyers. An economic rent for a three-roomed flat would be 16s 6d, with the Corporation contributing 6s.

Compulsory purchase orders for a site on the South Lotts Road in Ringsend were issued in early 1934, with an inquiry taking place in June and objections from the Pembroke Estate, which had planned to build ten houses on the site for £500 each. Simms told the inquiry that the cost of the proposed Corporation houses was £6,500; Pembroke Estate, which was worried about private enterprise taking over the site, had no objection to the Corporation's plans. A site on the North Lotts and another on Distillery Road, Drumcondra, which included the grounds of Strandville Football Club, were also subject to an inquiry, with Simms noting the keen demand from industry for factory sites in the area.

With garden-suburb ideals still firmly entrenched, the estates of Cabra and Crumlin were taking shape, although clearly the highest of design standards were difficult to maintain when top priority was providing the most housing possible at cheap prices. The two-storey 'cottages' were plain and utilitarian, though not without a certain austere elegance. Three house types were developed: Mk 1, a two-bedroom mid-terrace house, Mk 2, a three-bedroom mid-terrace house and Mk 3, an end-of-terrace house, which usually had three bedrooms. Built of concrete with a roughcast wall finish and painted in standard colours with well-designed doors and windows, these rows of similar houses made for coherent streetscapes. Sadly, much of the coherence has long since gone thanks to later modifications by owner-occupiers.

By 1935 the city manager was asking the question: how do you house the man who has no money? Four years after the launch of the Corporation's Housing Department, Simms told a 1936 tribunal into the rents paid by urban tenants that 'they were now trying to do in one generation what should have been done by the last four or five generations'. As well as negotiating funding and dealing with materials and labour shortages, Simms had to steer a course between the garden-suburb ideals of the city architect's office and the more militant views of the Housing Committee, which supported the building of inner-city block flats, the lowest possible rents and the clearing of the slums.

Despite the obsession with suburban estates, some twenty-one flat schemes designed by Simms and his team were completed between 1932 and 1950, with the best of them built before 1940. Although they reflected trends in Britain, the Netherlands and Austria, Dublin's four-storey blocks were unique in their density of forty flats to the acre and 24 per cent site coverage. In Britain, five-storey blocks were more common, making the density sixty flats per acre with 33 per cent coverage. While the overall design of the blocks recalled Dutch architect Michel de Klerk's projects in the 1910s, the deck access at the rear, which gave each flat its own front door, was closer to British schemes such as Tabard Gardens, China Walk Estate and Comber Estate in London. Yet, although clearly influenced by the London blocks and perhaps by Lancelot Keay, Simms' counterpart in Liverpool who favoured the use of brick and large windows, the Simms flats hinted at Dutch expressionism, notably the work of Piet Kramer, as well as de Klerk. Projected balconies with rounded corners, brick buildings facing existing streets, horizontal lines and arched entrances were expressionist features all faithfully followed in Dublin schemes, although the social philosophy behind the Dutch projects was absent.

With sites proving tricky and building costs high, Simms developed a general style for his block flats from the 1930s. Most were four- or five-storey blocks lining an existing street perimeter-style. Although modern, they echoed the classic style of the Georgian terraces for which the city was renowned. Thanks to their understated quality, they revitalised the neighbourhoods of Chancery Place, Marrowbone Lane, Henrietta Street and Townsend Street.

Overall, the design depended entirely on the site. Flat blocks could face each other across a courtyard, as at Henrietta House, or could intersect at corners to provide a clear perimeter, as in the Pearse House and Countess Markievicz House schemes. Some were linked at hinge points with long terraces and street fronts, as at Poplar Row and later at Marrowbone Lane. Larger sites, such as Oliver Bond Street, provided the opportunity to fold ranges back into the site creating squares and gardens. All the Simms inner-city schemes are built slightly off the street line behind iron railings and a grass strip. Most importantly, they respected their locations in low-rise Dublin.

6

The Housing Crisis Reaches a Peak

In 1935 Simms made trips to Germany and to Kenya, and in July he attended the International Housing and Town Planning Congress, held in London. Organisers were the International Federation for Housing and Planning, founded by Ebenezer Howard, the originator of the garden-city concept. With the emphasis firmly on garden suburbs and cities, the delegates heard papers on various topics, including the rehousing of tenants, rents, overcrowding, equipment and fittings, and public utility societies. Under the heading of 'Positive Town Planning' came papers on the deadweight of inertia, planning for decentralisation, aviation and electrification. A tour taking in Letchworth and Welwyn Garden

City was organised. Wherever he travelled, Simms took photographs of buildings that interested him.

The Irish census of 1936 showed that the housing crisis was reaching its peak, with 20,000 dwellings still needed in Dublin alone. In a busy year, a number of flat-block schemes were completed. With public interest in the housing crisis at a peak, the *Irish Press* began a campaign highlighting the appalling conditions endured by slum-dwellers in Ireland's large towns and cities. After noting that, despite eleven inquiries in the previous 138 years, nothing much had changed, the newspaper's editor, William Sweetman, argued that the slums were a legacy of British occupation.

On 3 November 1936 the newly-formed Citizens' Housing Council, which included church leaders and physicians, challenged prominent Dubliners to visit the slums. It published a report in 1937, praising the Corporation for its 'soundly and solidly built' flats and houses, but criticising it for neglecting to provide open spaces, playing fields and recreation areas along with schools and community centres. Dublin Corporation responded in 1938 with a report of its own, emphasising the cyclical nature of overcrowding in the tenements. As soon as one family was moved from a room it was re-let to another family, which may start small but usually expanded with the arrival of more children. With the population of Dublin unlikely to decrease, the problem seemed intractable.

Work continued in the Housing Architect's Department. In the north inner city, Avondale House on North Cumberland Street, off Parnell Street, was a neat development of three blocks around an entrance court-yard. It provided sixty-six flats and included a Penny Dinner hall. Facing the south bank of the River Liffey, St Audoen's House was a single block of fifty-five flats run-ning along Cook Street, which turned the corner onto Bridge Street Lower with an eye-catching clock tower and entrance. The tower has some fine brick detailing.

Largest of the earlier schemes was the Oliver Bond development, stretching over seven acres of the former Anchor brewery site off Bridgefoot Street and Usher's Quay, which was cleared in May 1933. Of the 391 flats in thirteen blocks eventually completed in 1936, 250 were two-bedroomed, with a scullery. In the main room was a cooker and a bath that, when covered by a hinged lid, served as a dining table. A further 130 flats had a single bedroom, while four were three-bedroomed and four were single-room bedsits. Also on the site were three houses for live-in caretakers, and children's play-grounds. Making a private inspection of the scheme in June 1935 was the papal nuncio, Most Reverend Paschal Robinson, along with the Minister for Local Government, Seán T. O'Kelly.

While enduringly popular with residents, who worked locally in clothing factories as well as in the Guinness brewery and Jameson distillery, the Oliver Bond scheme came in for some criticism. In the Dáil, James Dillon, who visited the flats in 1937, found the exterior attractive, but the rooms in the flats small and 'deplorably dark and dank'. Every flat should have a decent-sized living room, he argued. Although the Corporation had aimed to make about 70 per cent of its dwellings four-roomed, the real figure was closer to half. The Citizens' Housing Council echoed Dillon's views; the flats were substantially built and excellent in appearance, but why spend large sums on flats with rooms smaller than they should be? Comfort and space were increasingly in demand.

Compulsory purchase orders for land in Terenure and Harold's Cross Road were the subject of an inquiry in May 1936, which dealt with a number of objections from local residents as well as from the holders of ninety-eight allotments. Already ten of the 40 acres sought had been relinquished because of objections. At the inquiry, Simms pointed out that since the city's population was steadily expanding, the Dublin housing problem was not going to go away. Although the Corporation currently had contracts out for 2,300 dwellings on a tentative scheme of about 478 acres in the Crumlin area and also on 79 acres in central areas, they still needed the land in Terenure, where it proposed building 223 houses for better-off tenants. In relation to 18 acres in Harold's Cross, the Poor Clare Nuns were assured that only two rather than five acres of their land would be taken over, with a boundary wall to be erected between the building site and the convent.

In July 1936 Gerald Sherlock retired as city manager and was replaced as acting city manager by John P. Keane, until then the Corporation's financial adviser and the favourite for the job. Following a dispute with the Local Appointments Commission in 1937, Keane was replaced by ex-Dublin Commissioner Patrick Hernon, who took over as city manager with an annual salary of £1,700. He would control Dublin Corporation for many years.

Property rights were enshrined in de Valera's 1937 Irish Constitution, which included a guarantee that the Irish Free State would never pass a law 'attempting to abolish the right of private ownership, or the general right to transfer, bequeath or inherit property'.

From 1935 to 1938, the Local Government (Dublin) Tribunal, presided over by the barrister George Gavan Duffy, examined the possibility of a single council for County Dublin, as well as plans for managing the city's growth. On 20 July 1936 at a meeting of the tribunal, the city manager ordered Simms, along with the housing engineer P.E. Mathews, to submit a report on the preparation of a town-planning scheme. Headings were to include roads, housing schemes, general town-planning principles, open spaces, building densities and the advisability of zoning.

Following a preliminary report, Patrick Hernon decided that Simms should accompany him to England to obtain practical information from that country's experience of building social housing schemes and, in

particular, to assess the progress made in preparing planning schemes for built-up areas in cities.

Simms had already put the case for establishing satellite towns on the periphery of the city, garden-suburb
style, to the tribunal. He proposed locating industries
which would provide jobs in satellite towns and a 'green
belt' three-quarters of a mile deep at a radius of four
miles from the centre of the city. He argued that the
scheme was not so fantastically idealistic as some of its
critics had maintained. For instance, to the north, in the
Phoenix Park–Drumcondra outer segment of the city, the
Phoenix Park, Glasnevin Cemetery, the Botanic Gardens
and the Albert College farms were already established
open spaces and, if linked with adjoining agricultural
lands, could form the 'green belt barrier' for that section.

The present city boundary zigzagged in a random
fashion, with Inchicore one example. Since Dublin could
not continue spreading indefinitely, some form of decentralisation would eventually be necessary. Eight million
people at one time had lived in Ireland and that figure
would probably be reached again. Simms blamed the
slum crisis on neglect over three or four generations. He
believed that an intensified housing programme over a
number of years would sort out the main problems. After
that, housing should become a routine matter and not an
ongoing headache for future generations.

He believed that schools should be built in new areas
at the same time as houses: in one district on the outskirts

of Dublin where there were no schools, children were running wild. Religious leaders believed that they should be involved in such decisions and Simms admitted that in Crumlin, a plan for building a church and schools was made without consulting the relevant ecclesiastical authorities. As long as his overall plan was not frustrated, he accepted that the Catholic Church should have a say when it came to locating churches.

Following his appearance at the tribunal, Simms visited Austria and Hungary. In August 1936 he was in England where, as proposed by the tribunal, he examined housing schemes in several large cities. Travelling with him to England were P.E. Mathews, and J.P. Fitzgibbon of the Streets Department, who was the acting secretary of the Corporation's Town Planning Committee.

In Austria, 65,000 houses were built in Vienna at a rate of 5,000 houses a year in a city with a population of about a million. To allow for this significant building programme, private building was halted. The Catholic Party was now building at a rate of 750 dwellings a year, most in three-storey flat blocks with a balcony approach, which they had discovered was an old Viennese tradition. The schemes were called 'asylums for the poor' and many occupants were unemployed. In Budapest, all building was carried out by private enterprise, with no municipal involvement; existing one-storey cottages were replaced with blocks of four-storey flats. As for cross-Channel schemes in large cities, carrying out such schemes in Dublin would probably take years if not decades. In Birmingham, a scheme started in 1909 remained incomplete.

When it finally reached its conclusions, the Local Government (Dublin) Tribunal recommended that the greater Dublin area form one local administrative area with a detailed plan and a land-requisition policy taking account of future needs. In areas where schemes were proposed, the adjoining region must be considered; this had already happened in the case of housing schemes located between Kimmage and Crumlin.

While in England, J.P. Fitzgibbon had interviewed Patrick Abercrombie and Sydney Kelly, two of the three architects who had produced the 1914 plan for Dublin, and invited them to make a return visit to Dublin to discuss a revised city plan. Among those meeting them at City Hall on 18 September 1936 were Simms, Fitzgibbon and Mathews as well as the city manager.

Abercrombie and Kelly, accompanied by Fitzgibbon, Mathews and Simms, later made a tour of Dublin housing schemes, with Abercrombie professing himself astounded with the progress made. In his view, the present programme of building 2,000 houses a year put Dublin ahead of similar schemes in any English city of the same size. Along with the many inner-city clearances, this gave Dublin an opportunity to plan for the future. Since this could not be done in the course of a year, his advice was 'to go slowly and carefully'. He hoped to have a preliminary report prepared by the end of the month, with the finished plan to be completed with as little delay as possible.

In late October 1936 the Thorncastle estate in Ringsend, one of the 'unsanitary areas' covered by the Corporation's compulsory purchase orders, came up for discussion when the Dublin Housing Inquiry resumed in the City Hall with Denis Hickie of the Local Government Board supervising. Reflecting public interest in social housing at the time, the inquiry received a full-page spread in the *Irish Press* of 23 October.

Councillor Maud Walsh, speaking of conditions in Pembroke generally, said that families of six to ten were living in single tenement rooms: 'They are nearly in despair of being properly housed and have reached the stage of losing patience with their public representatives – and I don't blame them.' A small percentage of the existing tenants were waiting to be accommodated in Kimmage, but most of them refused to leave the district on the grounds of inconvenience and the cost of transport. The sixty-four new dwellings in Thorncastle Street, while welcome, were only a drop in the ocean. She blamed the housing problems on a set of officials in the Corporation for whom the housing problem had become 'a personal matter'.

Facing the Dodder river as it entered the Liffey at Grand Canal Docks in Ringsend, the Thorncastle Street scheme consisted of three blocks of flats. Work started in

1936 with the final block finished in 1939. With windows on its curved corners, the end block, located closest to Bridge Street, which was built first, was the most striking of the three.

On a compulsory purchase order for 246 acres in North Crumlin, a speculative builder objected that the value of the houses he was proposing to build on Herberton Road would deteriorate if inferior Corporation houses were built on the road. Simms argued that the Corporation was improving the neighbourhood; not causing it to deteriorate. Other objections came from the Meath Estate over the loss of playing fields. Simms replied that 76 acres were set aside for parks in Crumlin, while in the city itself they were attempting to bring nature back. For every 1,000 people the planners aimed to set aside five acres for parks, commons and open spaces and a further seven acres for playing fields in any scheme.

Facing the loss of 28 acres from its 112-acre site for future road-building was the Dublin Brick Company, based in Dolphin's Barn. Simms assured them that the Corporation had no intention of putting the Dublin Brick Company out of business. Also affected were the Grand Canal Company, and a 'carrier' for Guinness, based in Tara Street, which had about forty-five horses stabled on a one-acre site beside the owner's own home, Springfield House. A compulsory order relating to Newmarket, Marrowbone Lane and James's Street was also considered, with objections from a maltsters and from a local business at Blackpitts.

In January 1937 tenders were sought by the borough surveyor, Norman Chance, for 309 houses in Terenure's designated housing area. Croydon Park in Marino still required attention, with Simms designing railings and gates for tennis courts in July 1937. Later that year, work began on 182 four-roomed houses at the Ellenfield site on the Swords Road.

That same year Seán T. O'Kelly, the Minister for Local Government, called for the elimination of flats with fewer than three rooms and, as a result, the first section of the Sheriff Street scheme was adjusted to contain 128 four-roomed flats and 448 three-roomed flats, as well as a maximum of thirty-two shops. That meant sixty-four fewer flats than the 567 planned for originally. Around the same time, the Rialto and Donore Avenue schemes were also adjusted; Rialto would have two five-roomed, 147 four-roomed and 240 three-roomed flats, while Donore would have a single five-roomed flat along with 164 four-roomed, 361 three-roomed and only twenty-six two-roomed. Yet, as Simms knew very well, there was a demand for smaller units for families of two or three, and for those who could not afford high rents. Of the 367 families recently transferred, over a third wanted three rooms or fewer.

Development at Crumlin was continuing. The initial plans for the area dated back to the 1920s when the drains were laid. In August 1934 almost a hundred hectares of land were acquired for the sum of £55,158 and the construction of over a thousand two-storey houses in the four sections of what was called Crumlin South was soon underway.

Halting progress was the 1937 builders' strike, which began on 13 April and endured until October. At the time of the stoppage, the Corporation had building schemes in progress on cottage schemes in Crumlin, Terenure and Harold's Cross and on flats at Railway Street, Townsend Street, Aldborough House, Watling Street, Poplar Row, Henrietta Street and Thorncastle Street.

Plans to start work on 453 houses at Crumlin North, as well as at a section of Crumlin South and Emmet Road and on more flats at Railway Street were delayed. In order to keep vital work on Corporation schemes going during the strike, the Corporation asked Seán T. O'Kelly to sanction the use of direct labour for the Ellenfield and Larkhill schemes, both on the Swords Road. After receiving no reply, Thomas Kelly, chairman of the Corporation's Housing Committee, proposed that they set up their own building department. Workers employed by public and semi-public bodies would remain in their employment on the instructions of their trade unions. The strike finally ended on 3 October after long and arduous negotiations by Seán Lemass, the Minister for Industry and Commerce. It would take some time for the building trade to recover and only 200 Corporation dwellings were completed that year.

Soon after, compulsory purchase orders for a site in Cabra West, which would contain 1,950 houses, and for Donnycarney with plans for 1,032 houses, were confirmed. Flats were planned for a site in Rathmines.

In early October 1937 objections to an ambitious building scheme planned for Donore Avenue and Old County Road in Crumlin were heard, with Simms again cross-examined. In this area, close to the city centre, the plan was to build between 500 and 600 flats at a cost of £250,000. Replying to one objector who planned to build two shops on part of the site, Simms said that, in his opinion, the area was already 'over-shopped'. Losing the site would hamper the Corporation's plans to accommodate 2,500 people in a number of four-storey blocks, with open spaces and children's playgrounds also planned for. No new schools were needed since the Synge Street schools were only a quarter of a mile away.

On Wednesday 6 October, after giving his evidence to the inquiry, Simms spoke at a lecture held at the Society of Friends' meeting house in Eustace Street, presided over by the educationalist Isabel Douglas. Dublin architect George Beckett suggested that, despite splendid work in recent years, the increasing population was absorbing all Dublin's new houses, leaving the slum problem untouched. He wondered why the building strike was allowed to drag on when half the Corporation's annual programme remained unfulfilled.

In reply, Simms said that his main worry was whether the building trade could cope with plans to build 2,500 flats and 3,000 suburban houses. If these were to be turned into bricks and mortar, more tradesmen were needed to undertake the work. A short film showing the progress made by the Corporation in building housing over the previous ten years was shown.

By October 1937 the housing architect's staff included architects Charles McNamara and Donald Tyndall, engineer Edward Bourke, draughtsman and architect Timothy Ahern, Noel Taylor, P.J. O'Hare, V.S. Kilmartin, G.M. Costello, H. Stafford and D. Darker. At the end of that year, Dublin Corporation's debt stood at £8.9 million, of which £5.6 million related to its housing projects.

Tenders were invited for the Larkhill estate of 537 four-roomed houses and an estate-office annexe in April 1938 and for sixty-two four-roomed houses and a children's playing ground at a site between Emmet Road and Bulfin Road in June 1938; at Emmet Road, nothing much happened for the next two years when tenders were again invited.

Because of the prolonged builders' strike, only Emmet Buildings on Watling Street and Pearse House at Hanover Street were completed by 1938. In that year the Corporation considered putting central heating in its flat blocks for the first time, despite the medical officer's reservations – he felt central heating was unhealthy.

As it happened, putting in central heating would cost 6s 8d to 13s 7d per flat, which proved too expensive. Flats were heated by a range in the living rooms, a gas fire in the principal bedroom and sometimes a fireplace in the second bedroom. Coal was delivered through chutes into each flat from the access decks.

In April 1938 the newly-installed city manager Patrick Hernon promised that most of the 3,029 dwellings currently underway would be completed by year's end. An inquiry at City Hall on compulsory purchase orders began by looking at a 97-acre site at Rutland Avenue, which was an extension of the Crumlin development and part of Hernon's updated five-year plan recently adopted by the Corporation. The site in question consisted of 103 houses in poor condition; the families to be dispossessed would be accommodated in the adjoining housing area.

Towerfield House, a dairy farm in Dolphin's Barn, stood to lose 15 acres, which the owners regarded as essential to their business. Simms, who had already inspected the site, said that the land formed one of the biggest 'takes' of virgin land and was essential to the scheme. The owners of Dolphin Park Racing and Amusements, who had been making plans for the country's first pony-racing track in the area, were seeking an alternative site, as was a local pub bought in 1935.

At Larkhill, a contract for a further 537 houses to be completed by the end of the year would be placed in about a month's time, the inquiry heard. At that time, about 2,600 men were working on Corporation housing schemes and this number would increase.

Donnycarney, where a scheme of 1,000 houses was planned at a cost of £500,000, was the next subject of an inquiry in late August 1938. Local residents, who felt that the value of their properties, held under lease, had dropped, were looking for £200 compensation each. Simms, after explaining the Corporation's plans in detail, said that because the price of building materials had risen in recent times, it might not be possible to erect houses to the same standard as those already built. The Corporation agreed to build a nine-foot wall between its scheme and two other estates and to construct their best possible type of house on the Malahide Road frontage.

At an inquiry into the purchase of a 12-acre site at Watling Street, Simms said that the preliminary layout plan tentatively provided for 348 flat dwellings in three four-storey blocks. Based on Cook Street, built between 1934 and 1937, the estimate for building alone would have to be considerably increased to represent present-day costs. Not included in the estimate were acquisition costs, initial demolition, salvage of materials and the construction of any new or widened roads and public footpaths. Michael O'Brien, the Corporation's acting town-planning officer, approved the scheme. There were about thirty objectors.

By November 1938 the Anglican bishop Benjamin John Plunket had sold the St Anne's Park estate of 445 acres in Raheny to Dublin Corporation. Plunket had inherited the estate, formerly the residence of his uncle, Lord Ardilaun, following the death of Lady Ardilaun in 1937 but could not afford to keep it, although he held on to Sybil Hill and 30 acres as his residence. A plan to build about 3,000 houses was later abandoned in favour of creating a public park.

In 1939 Simms was elected a member of the RIAI. He was proposed by John Joseph Robinson and seconded by Richard Cyril Keefe and Harry Allberry.

A total of six flat schemes were completed in 1939, providing 712 flats. Among them were Ballybough House at Poplar Row, Liberty House at Railway Street, Countess Markievicz House on Townsend Street, St Joseph's Mansions in the gardens of Aldborough House on Portland Row and Henrietta House off Henrietta Street.

Not all schemes won approval. A suggestion for smaller flats on a site between Charles Street and Chancery Place, close to the quays, was rejected on the grounds that they would create further slums. As it happened, the Iveagh Trust was providing single-room accommodation locally, so the need was partly met.

The Corporation was well aware of the problems it still faced in housing the poor. In 1938, 1,445 families were living in stinking basements, 9,403 in crumbling tenements and 2,257 in unfit cottages. A further 6,768 lived in overcrowded conditions although the dwellings were otherwise in good condition. Some 17,000 families needed rehousing, yet finding homes for 12,000 was the best the Corporation could do with the available resources. Building 5,000 dwellings a year, as proposed by the Citizens Housing Council, was simply not possible. The Corporation was squeezed on costs for many reasons – new flats cost £875 and a cottage £663 to build and state subsidies came nowhere near covering the costs. Rents, which had been half the economic rent before, were now a third of that rate.

Yet in the 1930s, the Corporation was the most active builder in the city, constructing 2,500 more dwellings than the private sector and public utility societies combined: 7,637 dwellings compared to 5,173. It was no mean achievement.

7

The 1939 Inquiry

In February 1939 Dublin Corporation was criticised by T.F. Laurie, president of the Chamber of Commerce, for educating those who could well afford to pay an economic rent on how to negotiate a cheap rent at other people's expense.

The occasion was an official inquiry at City Hall into the Corporation's compulsory purchase of property on a half-acre site in the Bull Alley area off Patrick Street.

Thomas Kelly, head of the Housing Committee, vigorously defended the Corporation's record. 'The vast majority of the people housed by the Corporation are poor and cannot afford to pay an economic rent,' he said, inviting Laurie to make an inspection of some of the estates. He pointed out that since April 1935, 5,012 houses had been completed, 2,392 more were under construction and contracts for a further 1,500 were about to be issued. Schemes at Cabra and Crumlin and at Donore Avenue, Rialto and Emmet Road in Inchicore would provide a further 4,000 homes. He feared that Laurie's statement would deter better-off Dubliners from subscribing to future Corporation loan appeals.

Simms, who was present at the inquiry, added that from the zoning and town-planning perspective, there was no objection to the scheme for a block of flats on the opposite side of the road to the Iveagh Trust buildings. Some road-widening work would be necessary.

Not everyone thought the Corporation was doing a good job. In a letter to the *Evening Herald*, published on 4 February, 1939, an anonymous member of the RIAI wrote that the figures were nothing to boast about. 'At this rate of progress, thousands of poor people can only hope to leave the tenements in a coffin,' he wrote, calling for an official inquiry into the cost of constructing the average Corporation house.

With the Corporation's flat blocks, the cost could be reduced and the appearance of the building enhanced 'if the unnecessary ornament and fancy brickwork were omitted'. He argued that the Corporation was only 'picking' at the problem. 'If they cannot get enough money, let them build cheaper,' he argued. He suggested trying out other methods of construction and looking for outside help. 'As far as I know, the Institute of Architecture and other interested bodies had never been consulted.'

Seán T. O'Kelly, as Minister for Local Government and Public Health, agreed that an inquiry into the Dublin housing question was needed. Despite a disappointing response from interested parties and worries over the looming world war, the proposed inquiry went ahead, holding its preliminary sitting in the City Hall on 19 April 1939. Michael Colivet, the Department of Local Government's general inspector of housing, was the chairman. Making up the inquiry were Thomas Johnson, who was a Labour Party member of the Housing Board, along with T.C. Courtney and H.S. Moylan from the Department of Local Government and Public Health, and J.E. Hanna from the Department of Finance. The inquiry would meet at City Hall from April 1939 until late January 1940 with Simms called to give evidence several times and every possible aspect of Dublin's housing crisis forensically examined.

Amid a suspicion that some contractors were making exorbitant profits during a boom period for public housing, the primary function of the inquiry was to ascertain whether ratepayers and taxpayers were getting value for their money. From 1931 to 1938, just three contractors had divided over 82.7 per cent of tenders between them, although no concrete evidence pointed to price-fixing between the larger contractors.

At the first full meeting of the inquiry on 27 April, the Dublin city manager, Patrick Hernon, took three hours to deliver a summary of the situation. With some 22,000 still

117

living in unfit homes, the Corporation had come up with a ten-year plan for building 2,000 dwellings a year. That would bring its total debt to £22 million. The cost of labour and materials had risen steeply and was likely to continue rising. Within the previous few days, the Corporation had floated a loan for financing current schemes.

In response to Hernon's address, the Corporation's 'undue predilection for great blocks of flats on central city sites' was criticised, while Councillor James Larkin said that the allocation of houses was the greatest abuse in the state, with well-paid individuals getting houses ahead of families with six and seven children.

At the next meeting on 17 May, the inquiry looked into the problems of 'de-tenanting' areas scheduled for demolition. Priority for new housing was given to larger families living in tenements with staircases so steep that carrying children was a hazard or where rat infestation was a problem. Families with one or more members suffering from tuberculosis and families where the breadwinner was a night worker were next on the list.

A week later Hernon outlined the relative costs of cottages and flats. While flat blocks might be more expensive to build, the fact remained that not everyone wanted to move into the new housing estates far removed from the city centre:

We have had cases of people who have been delighted to get Corporation cottages at Crumlin and, after a time, have been appealing to get back into the city because they cannot pay the high transport charges and are unable to feed themselves. Without the Corporation transferring them at all, many of these people have gone back to rooms in the city equivalent to those from which they had been removed.

Because many tenants could not afford to pay their rent, the Corporation was experimenting with an 'incremental' system based on the tenant's circumstances. If the building programme was to continue, subsidies from both the Corporation and the state were essential.

At the next few sessions, Herbert Simms was giving evidence as the city's housing architect. Many of the dangerous buildings that they were demolishing, although probably not built to current standards, had nevertheless stood for 200 years; the only reason they were being pulled down was that they were neglected and not properly maintained. Building houses that lasted only fifty years would mean having to rebuild every fifty years, he pointed out. He agreed with the chairman's statement that what you save by cutting building costs, you lose ten times over in maintenance fees. They had experimented with paring down specifications, but after a few years they raised them again.

Speaking on the quality of the Corporation buildings, he said that while 'jerry-builders' had always existed, current building practices were more scientific, using a greater variety of materials and sounder construction methods. He believed that brick or cut stone was the only type of finish appropriate for city buildings and that, in the long run, it was cheaper to build brick buildings; indeed the German city of Hamburg had experimented with other finishes and ended up using brick. Careful town planning when building streets was essential, taking into account the social and aesthetic needs of the local community as well as individual requirements. Direct labour, which was used at Ellenfield and Larkhill on the Swords Road during the 1937 builders' strike, was proving more costly than contract work.

John Burke, Simms' assistant, when questioned on the use of timber in building, replied that, although in theory timber was cheaper, in practice it required constant maintenance and brought with it its own problems. A proposal to erect temporary wooden structures for slum-dwellers was rejected as wasteful since they, along with their concrete foundations and plumbing, would have to be cleared away after more permanent structures were built.

Simms was not entirely against some timber building, providing carpenters and joiners were readily available: 'I would recommend the building of red cedarwood houses, but limited in number to absorb only the fluctuating reserve of carpenters and joiners, though this type of construction would not absorb the usual quota per

St Michan's House – Simms' first solo effort.

Distinctive balconies at Mary Aikenhead House on Basin Street.

Pearse House, Hanover Street corner, soon after it was built.
(Courtesy of the G. & T. Crampton Archive.)

Pearse House today.

Chancery House beside the Four Courts in the 1930s.
(Courtesy of the G. & T. Crampton Archive.)

Chancery House today.

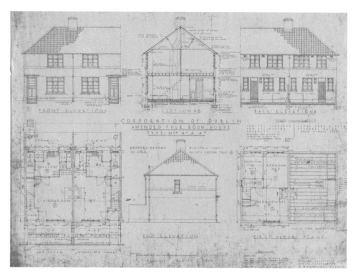

Standard Dublin Corporation plan for suburban house.
(Courtesy of the Irish Architectural Archive.)

A typical Crumlin estate.
(Courtesy of the G. & T. Crampton Archive.)

Markievicz House, Townsend Street.

Whelan House and O'Rahilly House facing
the Grand Canal Dock.

Emmet House on Watling Street.
(Courtesy of the G. & T. Crampton Archive.)

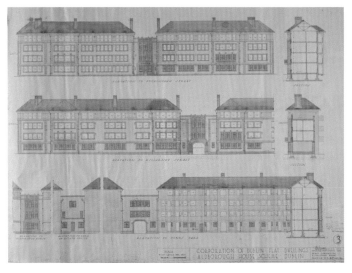

St Joseph's Mansions – the plan.
(Courtesy of the Irish Architectural Archive.)

St Joseph's Mansions soon after it was built.
(Courtesy of the G. & T. Crampton Archive.)

A refurbished St Joseph's Mansions; now called Killarney Court.

A panoramic view of the Fatima Mansions scheme.
(Courtesy of the G. & T. Crampton Archive.)

St Teresa's Gardens – the final farewell.

building of building labourers, of which there has always been a surplus supply.'

Re-examined by Thomas Johnson on housing costs, Simms said that the figures provided showed the worst side of the picture. Comparing type for type, the increase in costs since 1932 was 8 per cent and not roughly 45 per cent as had been maintained. Asked about the 16.7 per cent increase in costs ascribed to 'sundry unenumerated factors', Simms replied that he was told that this was for 'some other thing we don't know about'. He put it down to the use of less experienced contractors.

Simms referred to the report of the Scottish committee on building costs, which maintained that reduced productivity from labour was partly responsible for the increased cost of building houses. Such conditions possibly also existed in Dublin, but it was difficult to estimate whether reduced output increased building costs. He added that there was nothing to prevent contractors paying good workers more than the minimum, as was done in London. 'Some of those skilled masons get much more than the minimum for doing highly skilled and intricate work,' he said.

Disputes occurred in Dublin from time to time over the allocation of work. One of the most recent disputes concerned whether it was bricklayers or joiners who should fix steel windows. After a three-week delay came a decision to share the work.

Referring to Scottish measures to increase the supply of labour, Simms said that the lack of local plasterers had slowed down the building programme in Dublin on two occasions. Trade unions had been accused of refusing to accept new members, which Simms felt should not be a problem if a definite long-term building programme were adopted and work guaranteed.

When it came to building materials, the biggest problem was finding 'facing' bricks. Sporadic deliveries from 1937 to 1938 had coincided with the shortage of bricklayers. For roofs, Irish slates were put to limited use but even so, deliveries were not reliable. For large city schemes, interlocking machine-made concrete tiles were in general use. These were less expensive than slates and supplies were good.

Costs of building the four-storey flat blocks in Dublin had increased because of the larger size of dwellings in more recent schemes and the need to provide amenities such as sun balconies, pram and cycle garages, and children's playgrounds. Blocks of flats originally designed to contain only three-roomed dwellings were changed later to include flats with two, three and four rooms, as well as occasional single- and five-room dwellings, depending on planning and site requirements. As Simms explained:

> Some of our earlier flat schemes based on Department of Local Government and Public Health requirements had been described by one outside critic as 'dog boxes'. Notwithstanding

this expression of opinion, I am of the opinion that economies could be affected in future flat schemes by a reduction in the overall size of the dwelling as compared with some of our latest plans. Private sun balconies are additional attractions and serve practical purposes in the case of consumptive families, but owing to the extra cost, should be strictly limited to this use and not introduced as a general amenity.

Marrowbone Lane, a scheme of 112 flats then under-way, had no balconies. Simms believed that both flats and cottages had a place in any attempt to solve Dublin's housing problem; the Corporation's town-planning consultants agreed with him on that point. Although smaller flats did not pay their way, they were needed for the one-, two- and three-person families the Corporation had to house.

Housing the working classes would have to be accepted sooner or later as a permanent service, like water or other municipal services, Simms emphasised when continuing his evidence on 1 June.

In the past, providing this class of housing was treated as temporary work – something that could be done over, say, five years. Since the annual requirements might be 500 houses or more, or 300 or less, depending on demand, such rigid plans were not practical.

During the previous financial year, 2,336 dwellings were completed and no shortage of labour or materials experienced, thanks to a reduction in private building owing to the unsettled international conditions and the high cost of building. While that had helped Corporation contractors achieve a record output, the present unbalanced conditions would not remain forever.

Only with a reliable, long-term financial policy could progress be maintained. Restricting private building developments would be 'the biggest mistake that could be made' since the city needed an overall building programme, which would include private development. If anything was to be curtailed, that might be the building of 'luxury' amenities such as cinemas which, because they paid better wages, caused an occasional drop in the number of plasterers available to the Corporation.

Simms pointed out that every house provided by private builders and public utility societies helped ease the problem. A person who went into a £1,000 house usually left a £600 house vacant for somebody else. State assistance for private builders could help ease the housing crisis in an indirect way.

Questioned on the life of Corporation cottages and flats, he repeated his often-stated belief that if properly maintained, such buildings should last 200 years, which was longer than the life of the slum dwellings they were replacing. As to density of building, he suggested fifteen or sixteen cottages to the acre as the ideal and never more than eighteen. Flats varied in density from thirty to fifty an acre, and fifty flats could accommodate about 250 persons.

Building costs would not be reduced by giving out small contracts, he said, since the number of large, highly-organised contractors in Dublin was limited. Often only two tenders were received for a large contract. When the larger contractors had obtained enough work to keep them going, smaller contractors began competing for work. Only by increasing the number of apprentices or paying for overtime at normal rates could output be improved.

Simms said that because it was uneconomic to provide two-roomed flats with all the necessary services, only the minimum number of them should be built. From both the architectural and economic points of view, he would prefer not to build anything less than three-roomed flats and he agreed with the chairman that with flats of one or two rooms, questions of decency standards arose since the sexes had to be separated.

Suburban development was bringing with it new churches and schools, said Simms, adding that the centre of Dublin must be reconstructed for residential purposes. If this didn't happen, attendances at the churches and schools in the city itself would be affected.

On using cut stone for front door steps, Simms told the inquiry that the stones came in from the quarries and were then dressed by stonecutters, costing the

Corporation about £1 each – twice as much as when they were dressed in the quarries. The system helped relieve unemployment among city stonecutters which, as Colivet, the inquiry's president, put it, was another instance of housing carrying someone else's burden.

With a second world war looming, the prices of steel, timber and cement were increasing as the world's powers stocked up on arms, reported Simms, when continuing his evidence before the inquiry on 5 June. Ireland's policy of self-sufficiency was bound to result in higher costs and he noted that if each country finished its own products before trading them with other countries, costs would be much less. 'There is no reason why we should bear the costs of transporting useless sawdust in the raw wood purchased from Sweden,' he pointed out. Cement prices were affected not by international conditions but by regulation of the Irish cement industry, which had wiped out the local surplus. The cost of prepared timber in Ireland was 15 per cent higher than in England, although the bulk of timber was coming not from but through Britain to Ireland.

Simms agreed with the chairman that there could be an average saving of about 10 per cent by ordering directly from the manufacturers instead of through builders' providers, who – it was now agreed – had been operating a price-fixing ring since 1934. Most of the manufacturers were already contracted to deal with the builders' providers and there was nothing much that the Corporation or the builders could do about it. When the large contractors had dealt directly with English importers of timber some years earlier, the shipping companies refused to carry the orders. However, if Corporation schemes were placed in a special category, it could be feasible to make a saving by direct purchasing.

Having to use expensive Irish-manufactured goods was another factor that increased the cost of building prices, while imported goods were subject to hefty tariffs. Only recently the Corporation had paid half the price again in duty when importing children's playground equipment.

Simms thought that there was room for another brickworks in Dublin, since Dolphin's Barn brickworks had to ration supply to its customers. When queried on the possibility of using cheaper bricks, he argued that while Courtown facing brick was cheaper, it gave the ordinary reddish colour instead of the present multi-coloured, rustic effect. When it came to labour, the average hourly rate had gone up by tuppence since 1937 for labourers, bricklayers, stonecutters, tilers, plasterers, painters and glaziers, and by slightly more for plumbers and electricians.

In his next appearance before the inquiry on 16 June, Simms defended the higher cost of building flat blocks. It was not fair, he argued, to compare the price of city-centre flats with cottages in the suburbs without considering the increased cost to the taxpayer of transport and other public services when looking at suburban developments.

On the weekend of 24 June, Herbert Simms attended the Conference of the Royal Institute of British Architects at the RIBA headquarters on Merrion Square, Dublin, where Charles Herbert Aslin gave a lecture called 'The Work, Duties, and Responsibilities of the Official Architect'. The conference was held in Dublin as part of the Royal Institute of the Architects of Ireland centenary celebrations.

Official architects for cities were appointed at a time when governments were increasingly involved in providing social services, such as housing, libraries, police stations, hospitals and schools, Aslin said. In some cases, a surveyor or engineer employed architects to carry out the work. In other cases, projects for civic works were decided by public competitions. In proposing a vote of thanks to Aslin, Simms said that official architectural departments had become more common in the past twenty years; sometimes ousting brother professionals such as engineers 'who had been inclined to poach on architects' preserves to a far greater extent than was either reasonable or good'.

In the previous fifty to sixty years, the development of large-scale public works had increased the need for official departments; this led ultimately in an improvement in civic architecture and town planning. 'Official architects of large-scale planning works not only designed buildings as such but were also provided with opportunities to design whole street elevations; opportunities not often presented to most private practitioners,' said Simms, emphasising that an official architect should possess a competent knowledge of civic design.

In the article on 'Municipal Housing Activities' for the conference handbook, Simms wrote that the shortage of housing in Dublin 'appears to be probably greater than ever before in the history of the city'. People were expecting more from a dwelling than 'mere protection from the elements by four walls and a roof of some kind'. Looking at the history of public housing in Dublin, he remarked that only from 1925 was hot water and a bath supplied in each flat.

Back giving evidence to the Housing Commission, Simms summarised the reasons why the cost of building houses in Dublin had risen. New wage scales, more stringent conditions of employment, increased insurance bills, and the 35 per cent increase in the cost of building materials were the main factors.

Other contributors to rising costs included the scarcity of skilled labour and the lack of competition which, when work was plentiful, tempted contractors to increase their prices. Smaller contractors, with little experience of the work, could produce abnormally high tendering figures. Price-fixing between Dublin builders' merchants, which eliminated effective competition, was yet another cause of higher costs, as indeed was the larger size of the houses.

Because planning, design and specifications had changed, determining the causes of increased building costs was not simple. It would be difficult to find a single example of a Corporation house built in 1938 in accordance with exactly the same drawings and specification as four or five years earlier. The average cost for houses in Dublin varied from £279 in 1934 to £451 in 1938, an increase of 61.7 per cent. The corresponding figure for Scotland was 7.7 per cent.

Giving evidence on 6 July, Dr Robert Collis, representing the Citizens' Housing Council, said that a thousand babies died each year mainly because of the slum conditions they were born into. If a hundred babies died in a bombing raid there would be an outcry, yet there was no such outcry at a loss of ten times that figure. Society had become inured to such conditions.

While not critical of Corporation officials, who were dealing with a chronic lack of cash, Collis asked whether they had considered the big grievance of the building trade, which was the uncertainty of employment. There were also the practical problems of moving slum–dwellers to new settlements. Transport remained in the hands of a monopoly and the ready availability of essential amenities such as cheap shops, social centres and playing fields in the new settlements was not considered. Hundreds of recently moved families were clamouring to get back to the city centre. He believed that the policy of only moving large families into these estates had created artificial communities, while placing families stricken with tuberculosis in those settlements was dangerous and ill-judged.

In mid-July came a happier occasion when the Lord Mayor, Kathleen Clarke, officially opened a modern Child Welfare Clinic and Dining Hall at St Joseph's Mansions, Killarney Street, the first of its kind. At the reception Mrs Clarke opened the facility with a golden key presented to her by Simms on behalf of the contractors, G. & T. Crampton.

St Joseph's was just one of six schemes completed in 1939. They ranged in size from Henrietta House with forty-eight flats to Liberty House with 181 flats. Well underway was the Marrowbone Lane scheme, which backed on to the Guinness brewery, and Mary Aikenhead House at Basin Street off St James's Street. Both were completed in 1940.

Even after the Second World War was declared on 1 September 1939, the Housing Commission continued to sit when evidence from the Building Trades Group of the Dublin Trades Union Council was heard. James Larkin gave details of a direct labour housing scheme carried out for the Corporation, with 190 houses built for a cost of £93,000; a similar but smaller scheme built by a contractor had cost £95,000. While Larkin maintained that the houses built using direct labour at a much lower cost were

131

as good as any built by contractors, he agreed that strict supervision was essential. At Ellenfield, virtually all the doors had to be replaced when the wrong materials were used. For jobs in the suburbs, a big problem for workers was the oft-quoted cost of transport. Simms made a brief appearance when the subject of the gas fittings and bath and sink waste-pipe fittings used in Corporation dwellings came up. He made it clear that the Corporation had speci-fied first-class quality when looking for ball valves.

In a later session which, among other topics, looked at the possibility of cooking a pig's cheek, a head of cab-bage and half a stone of potatoes on the range provided in a Corporation dwelling, Simms suggested to the inquiry that tenants be shown how to use the ranges, the taps and the other fixtures in their new homes. Some tenants had removed the ranges because they preferred it when the living room, where the ranges were installed, looked more like a sitting room.

In mid-December Seán Milroy TD stated that the Corporation had neither the organisation nor the resources to grapple with the task of housing the poor. As things stood, the Corporation had reached a situa-tion where it was impossible to continue on present lines without exposing Dublin to financial breakdown, and yet it was equally impossible to slow down without aggravating enormous social evils.

That the number of dwellings unfit for human habi-tation in Dublin had risen from 6,831 in 1914 to 17,759 in 1939 was staggering. The government should consider balancing the increased cost of building materials against the sums of money it would have to pay out to support the unemployed if the building trade collapsed.

Referring to the shortage of skilled labour, Milroy said a member of the Dublin Vocational Education Committee had told him that the trades and the unions were restricting numbers enrolling in classes for the crafts.

James Hardress de Warrenne Waller, originator of the 'Angora' system of lightweight concrete construction, said that the Corporation should forget about building houses and strive to manufacture and assemble them. His system had been used by the Corporation in 1928 when building a street of two-storey flat-roofed houses in Rialto.

The Housing Commission held its final sitting in early 1940. Its recommendations when they finally came out were little more than a summary of housing legislation over the previous fifty years. It concluded that 22,872 houses were needed to solve the Dublin housing crisis. It offered no suggestions as to how this might happen.

8

The 'Emergency' and War Work

In July 1939 work on the housing schemes came to a halt when the city manager, Patrick Hernon, refused to sanction any further contracts until sufficient funding was found. The Corporation's attempt to raise funds by floating a loan of £1.5 million had proved less than successful: the public had been expected to subscribe about half of the fund – underwriters would cover the rest. The response had been sluggish to say the least. By mid-November a mere 400 or so men were working on building sites in the city, compared to about 2,300 in a good period. Between five and seven thousand men were out of work because of the building industry's downturn. On a positive note, the cost of building had dropped, with a contract for 500 cottages in Crumlin showing a reduction in price of between £80 and £90 for each cottage compared to a year earlier.

By the summer of 1939 it was clear that a world war was looming. Although Ireland would remain neutral during a period it called 'the Emergency', the Free State government initially believed that Ireland had little to fear because of its geographic location, with Germany about 800 miles distant. Even if Northern Ireland became a target, bombers would have to fly across England, braving searchlights, anti-aircraft guns and barrage balloons. No one was taking a chance, however, and on 26 July 1939 the Air Raid Precautions (ARP) Act became law, with local authorities receiving technical advice, special equipment and financial assistance.

To study ARP and emergency fire-fighting methods, Major J.J. Comerford, chief superintendent of Dublin Fire Brigade, travelled to England. Comerford had been appointed to the job after three firemen tragically died while attending a fire in Pearse Street in 1936. A survey of the fire service by Lieutenant Colonel Guy Symonds, fire adviser to the British Home Office, had followed and now Symonds was invited back to Dublin to advise the government on civil defence measures. Around the same time, an ARP branch of the Department of Defence (later called the Military Directorate of Civil Defence), headed by Colonel Seán O'Sullivan, was put in charge of drawing up and implementing plans relating to buildings, equipment, evacuation, training schemes and advisory services.

Heading up Dublin Corporation's ARP was Thomas Gay, its head librarian, with Herbert Simms delegated to look after the rescue and demolition services. In collaboration with the Master Builders' Association, Simms began organising 'light' and 'heavy' rescue groups in various parts of the city. Eleven 10-tonne jacks and two 20-tonne jacks along, with forty-four 10-foot rope ladders and other specialist equipment, were acquired and stored at the Housing and Maintenance Headquarters Depot in Keogh Barracks. A survey of houses located basements suitable for shelter in the event of an air raid. Some 360 Corporation employees received training in the Civilian Anti-Gas School at Griffith Barracks.

Around the country, air-raid shelters, sirens and emergency water tanks were installed, with volunteers recruited under a number of headings: auxiliary fire service (AFS), wardens, decontamination and casualty, and rescue and demolition. The primary duty of the volunteers was to enforce black-out regulations.

On 10 June 1939 Simms and other Corporation staff travelled to the Kilbride army camp in County Wicklow where a new Department of Defence-designed air-raid shelter was tested. This conical shelter was intended to protect up to six people from the impact of a 50-pound high-explosive bomb exploding 50 feet away. Subjected to three 'bombings' was a test group of three, including the Minister for Defence, Frank Aiken. Less than three months later, Germany invaded Poland and on 1 September 1939, Britain declared itself at war.

In January 1940 a Corporation meeting was asked to restore the bus services bringing children from the Ellenfield and Larkhill areas to their city-centre schools. At the same meeting, Simms was instructed to use wooden sashes instead of steel frames for the windows of houses in a new housing scheme at Crumlin. Simms had estimated that using steel frames would result in a saving of £1,226.

In February, after the Iveagh Trust had proposed transferring its flat blocks at Bellevue Buildings and Thomas Court to the Corporation, Simms and Charles McNamara inspected the properties accompanied by Joseph Sherwin, the assistant city manager, and another representative of the Corporation's Housing Department. With a number of councillors, they also visited the nearby Marrowbone Lane scheme, which was almost completed.

The suburban houses versus city-centre flats debate was reignited during the 1940s, although building low-density 'cottage' schemes in central areas was no longer considered an option. Despite the suburban estates not being popular with everyone, the Corporation pressed ahead with them during the Emergency. With funding scarce and building materials costly, they were viewed as the only option. Flat blocks needing strong foundations cost more to build and clearing sites was expensive. Yet when families were housed in the city, they could walk to work and could rely on the support of established local communities. Such factors were not considered.

On 29 February 1940 Simms made the news for non-architectural reasons when his house at 45 Mobhi Road Glasnevin, was broken into and jewellery worth about £30 taken. After failing to get into the house on the ground floor, the burglars had climbed a short drainpipe and entered through the bathroom. The house was ransacked, with drawers opened and their contents strewn about. Six houses on the road were burgled on the same night by a gang of three youths aged in their early twenties.

By 1940 the war was affecting the supply of building materials and the cost of a three-bedroomed house had jumped from around £800 to £1,500. In June of that year, Simms wrote to Joseph Sherwin about his Sheriff Street and Newfoundland Street designs, which pro-posed building 256 units in eight blocks. He had decided to limit small balconies to the corners of the buildings, where they served as outdoor bedrooms for consumptives. During this period, the office of the housing architect moved from 3 Parliament Street to 5 Wellington Quay.

A terrace of six houses in Crumlin North planned from late 1940 was only completed in April 1944 by the builders G. & T. Crampton. After starting the process of tendering, Simms had realised that the cost of each house's superstructure had increased by over two-thirds in less than six years owing to the rising prices of timber, steel and cement. In a list compiled for Joseph Sherwin,

Simms showed that a house in Crumlin North now cost £418 13s 1d to build, compared to £291 8s 40d in April 1934 for a scheme in Crumlin South, when Fearon Builders were the contractors.

Public utility societies were continuing to build houses for the private market with the Corporation providing assistance with site development and access to grants. In 1938, as part of a slum-clearance effort by the St Ultan's/Charlemont Public Utility Society, the modernist architect Michael Scott had been commissioned to build a flat block by the health reformer and 1916 veteran Madeleine ffrench-Mullen. Scott, often scathing in his criticism of the Dublin Corporation's housing projects, came up with a plan for an eight-storey building designed to form part of a much larger scheme. In the end, all that was built was a scaled-down four-storey block of thirteen flats lining the street. With its flat roof, box-like shape, two internal stairways, overhanging eaves, port-hole windows and balconies, it was clearly influenced by the German Bauhaus architect Walter Gropius.

Scott, during his periods as president of the RIAI in 1937/8, had brought Gropius to Dublin to present a lecture. He claimed that the German architect was horrified by the poor quality of recent Dublin buildings, in particular the Corporation flat blocks. By 1941, ffrench-Mullen House, as it was called, was ready for occupation. The entire Charlemont scheme was finally completed by Dublin Corporation in 1969.

In July 1940 Radio Éireann broadcast the first in a series of talks on ARP, with Patrick Hernon appealing for 2,000 volunteers to undertake various services and Simms suggesting that neighbours in suburban areas form groups to undertake rescue and demolition work if houses in their localities were hit during an air raid. 'The scheme looks simple in theory and it could be made simple in practice if people do not forget to be cool, calm and collected,' he told his radio audience. By the end of that month the city had 2,261 wardens with a further 530 undergoing training. Provision for forty-five overground shelters was made and four mobile units for the casualty service were almost ready. A decontamination centre at Stanley Street was complete, with a second centre ready to go. Ten centres opened to instruct the public in air-raid protection.

Simms began instructing members of the Dublin Building Trades Group in rescue and demolition work. At the Messrs Collins yard on East Wall on 27 September, Simms, with the depot supervisor, demonstrated ARP methods of 'shoring' dangerous walls and erecting barriers around areas where wrecked buildings might prove a danger to the public. At the G. & T. Crampton premises in Shelbourne Road, where Simms' colleague Noel Taylor was in charge, Éamon de Valera was shown how bombing victims could be rescued from under piles of debris using acetylene welding on steel girders and hoists to remove heavy rubble. Clearly the rescuers' work was both difficult and dangerous.

A total of 350 volunteers, selected for their skills in steel erection, lifting appliances, scaffolding, the use of explosives and building repairs, made up the rescue and demolition service. Squads were stationed in eleven area depots located in building contractors' yards in the city. In the case of a bombing, their primary tasks were to rescue people trapped in wreckage and to deal with dangerous water, gas and electricity leaks.

Two days later, on Sunday 29 September, some 6,000 ARP workers paraded through the streets of Dublin, starting at St Stephen's Green and finishing at Parnell Square, with thousands lining the route. Air-raid wardens, numbering some 1,700 men from the nine city wards, were at the head of the parade, followed by 300 women wardens. After that came fifty Dublin Fire Brigade members along with 300 recruits from the Auxiliary Fire Brigade. About 260 trained workers from the rescue and demolition service marched beside eleven fully-equipped rescue and demolition lorries.

Representing St John's Ambulance Brigade and the Red Cross were around 1,500 members, along with five buses that had been converted into mobile units. The decontamination service displayed three vehicles complete with crew and equipment, while also marching were 1,000 members of the emergency communications service.

In December 1940 Patrick Abercrombie was back in Dublin with a new sketch plan for the city. It proposed adopting controlled 'green belt' areas between the city proper and satellite towns. Dealing with criticisms that the new plan for Dublin would cost ratepayers a small fortune, Abercrombie replied that planning cost nothing. 'We do not suggest that you should spend anything, but merely indicate the lines on which you should proceed to get the best value for your money.' Herbert Simms backed him up: 'We'll be spending millions anyway in the course of the next few years. We must keep the building trade going, apart altogether from other and possibly more important considerations. We need advice to ensure that the citizens' money is not wasted.' Abercrombie, along with his colleagues, Sydney Kelly from Liverpool and local architect Manning Robertson, would remain in consultation with the Corporation until the planning scheme received parliamentary approval.

Despite Ireland's neutral status, German bombs had fallen on Terenure and the South Circular Road in Dublin in late 1940 and early 1941, as well as on a number of sites on the east coast where six people died, but no one was killed in Dublin. In the early hours of 31 May 1941, any pretence that Ireland was safe from the devastation of war ended when German aircraft were heard flying over Dublin city. Irish troops launched warning flares and anti-aircraft guns opened fire, without hitting the planes. In 37 minutes the Germans dropped four high-explosive bombs on the city, the first of them falling on the Ballybough area, demolishing two houses in Summerhill Park. Several people suffered injuries, but there were no deaths.

A second bomb fell at the pumping works near the zoo in the Phoenix Park, damaging windows at Áras an Uachtaráin, the official residence of President Douglas Hyde, while a third fell on the North Circular Road near Summerhill, causing no injuries. The largest and most destructive of the four bombs hit the North Strand area between the Five Lamps and Newcomen Bridge. At least thirty-four people died, with nearly a hundred more injured and almost 4,000 properties 'harmed'.

'It was just devastated – beds hanging out of the floors, curtains waving in the breeze, pictures wobbling on the walls, the whole front of the buildings gone,' said Alec King, head of the ARP depot in Ballsbridge, in an RTÉ broadcast from 1988.

As soon as it was possible, King and others began the harrowing and dangerous task of digging through the rubble in search of survivors, with Simms later praised for his cool-headed management of the operation.

Emergency shelter for survivors was provided by the Red Cross at its headquarters on Mespil Road as well as at the Mansion House and in parish halls throughout the city. Charleville Mall Public Library, located off the North Strand, became headquarters for the bombed area. Wherever possible houses were made good, and when property was damaged beyond repair, the occupants were offered compensation and moved to the housing estates of Cabra and Crumlin. Dublin Corporation acquired two areas where the bomb damage was most severe, one off Summerhill Parade and the other off the North Strand, where it proposed clearing the remaining buildings and developing a new housing scheme. Of the 4,000 damaged properties, the Corporation made 2,500 fit for habitation.

On Friday 6 June, when the funerals of twelve victims of the bombing took place at the St Laurence O'Toole church, ARP members wearing their helmets were part of the packed attendance. Leading the mourners was the Taoiseach, Éamon de Valera.

On 3 July Simms gave evidence at the inquest into three deaths following the collapse of a 180-year-old tenement house at Bride Street on the day after the bombing. The victims were Bridget Lynskey, her five-month-old son Noel, and Samuel O'Brien, aged seventy-two. A further eleven people were injured although six were quickly discharged from hospital, including the two other Lynskey children. Francis, their father, disclosed that on the day before the house collapsed, he had received the key for a house at Cooley Road in Crumlin. Simms and members of the ARP had arrived promptly at the scene, where Robert W. Hall was leader of the demolition squad. They managed to free two women from the rubble but could not save Mrs Lynskey. Later, one of the residents of 46 Bride Street would take an action against the minister for finance for loss of property. Simms was again called to give evidence and agreed that while the explosion was possibly the last straw, it was likely that the 180-year-old building had collapsed from old age.

Three days later, on Sunday 6 July, the first large-scale mobilisation of the Dublin City ARP services took place, based around an imagined bombing attack by fifty planes in which essential services were disrupted and much 'havoc' caused. Sirens sounded at 10.25 a.m. with the all-clear almost 90 minutes later. 'Bombed places' included Kingsbridge train station, tram sheds at Clontarf, both ends of Grafton Street and Westland Row. Controller of the exercises was Simms' architect colleague, Robert Lawrie, who was chief warden and ARP officer. Services in action included the Dublin Fire Brigade and the ARP rescue service led by Simms. Simms gave another Radio Éireann talk on 'rescue and demolition work' towards the end of July.

Thanks to the bombings, with thousands of slum-dwellers displaced, the housing situation in Dublin moved from ongoing problem to immediate crisis. Dublin Corporation began renovating suitable Georgian tenement buildings, acquiring them by compulsory order and moving out the tenants. A ten-roomed house in Sean McDermott or Lower Gardiner Street might be turned into four or five self-contained flats. Alfred William Maunsell Ternan, a trained engineer and building surveyor from Simms' department, was put in charge.

Buildings were stripped back, with a new concrete core inserted and the brick front re-proofed.

Reconditioning was deemed a success – as well as reducing density, it spared the city's Georgian heritage and kept inner-city communities intact. The interiors of the houses were drastically re-shaped, with new central light wells installed from roof to basement housing the water and drainage and the new bathrooms and kitchens grouped around them. Creative use was made of existing materials, with old railway lines adapted to make grates, and old window shutters becoming doors.

After the 1941 bombing, the Royal Institute of the Architects of Ireland (RIAI) called for an emergency meeting with the Corporation. At the time the RIAI was headed by William Cooke, who had enjoyed a long career with the OPW. A subsequent conference of the 'Emergency Housing Committee' in 1942 called for temporary dwellings, arguing that a three-roomed dwelling would cost only £250 to build although it would have no washing facilities. Simms told the attendance that the Corporation had a scheme in hand for 500 small one-storey dwellings, incorporating washing facilities. He refused to be pushed into building temporary or prefabricated dwellings. 'With the present scarcity of building materials, it behoves us to place what is available to the best possible use and not to waste the materials on erecting temporary buildings,' he said. In the 1940s prefabricated implied flimsy, although building methods were changing and the Crampton firm was developing pre-cast and ready-mixed concrete.

When the RIAI insisted that it wanted its members involved in housing design, the Corporation offered a compromise, suggesting the RIAI should canvass its members for ideas, with proposals to be forwarded to the department and exhibited at the forthcoming National Planning Exhibition in the Mansion House. Seeking a more radical approach to public housing, Seán MacEntee, Minister for Local Government and Public Health from 1941, while visiting the exhibition, proposed a planning board, with a housing programme among its responsibilities. His proposal was not successful. During the Emergency, the Minister for Industry and Commerce, Seán Lemass, headed a temporary Department of Supplies, which evolved into a division of the Department of Industry and Commerce after the war and attempted to co-ordinate the planning of all building activities.

From 1941 Simms and the contractors employed by the Corporation juggled with materials in an effort to keep projects moving. Building had begun on Dolphin Terrace, a cottage scheme at 45–50 Dolphin Road, with Charles Ashworth and Simms himself the architects and Crampton's the builders. To cut costs, timber ceiling joists were placed fifteen rather than fourteen inches apart, while timber sheeting was replaced with plasterboard, and stained brown linoleum or screed concrete used instead of timber on the floors. Half an inch was pared off the standard two-inch internal doors, although when Patrick Hernon, the city manager, suggested that they skimp on skirting boards, Simms refused.

Electrical cable was in short supply and to avoid laying off skilled labour, Simms proposed leaving traps in the floors to allow the wiring to be completed later. He was putting only three electrical points in a four-roomed house, since strict limits on British imports meant neither switches nor holders were available. Seán Moylan, then parliamentary secretary to the Department of Industry and Commerce, later Minister for Lands, would lobby on behalf of the Corporation for building materials as the crisis deepened.

By February 1942, Crampton's could not get the two tonnes of sheet lead it needed from the British Lead Mining Company to complete the project. When Moylan suggested using Ruberoid felt as an alternative, Simms expressed his reluctance to use such an inferior material for chimney flashing. He suggested that the department ask the Mining Company of Ireland to obtain pig lead from England. He received a non-committal response. The next crisis was the lack of petrol, which meant the Corporation could not use the standard two-and-a-half-tonne rollers when making footpaths. It was forced to fall back on a mechanical rammer, which almost guaranteed that cracks would appear sooner rather than later. Although the contract for building the houses was signed in 1943, the terrace was not ready for occupation until April 1944.

In a letter to Joseph Sherwin, Simms wrote:

All public services are complete with the exception of the gas branch supply pipe from main to houses. [There are no] pokers, rakes, or flue brushes to ranges. Single or twin single or triple revolving coat hooks for presses no longer available. Wood stops fixed at skirting for hall doors in lieu of rubber stops, which are now unattainable. There is a single wire and iron dividing fence in rere [sic] gardens in lieu of two-bar fencing. No picture hangers. No curtain rail fixed in living room between door to hall and rere porch.

Such was his attention to detail.

St Mary's Mansions at Sean McDermott Street, with ninety-four flats, was completed in 1942 and Simms continued to work on flat schemes for Newfoundland Street, Railway Street, Donore Avenue and Rialto. The Donore Avenue and Rialto schemes showed a shift away from inner-city locations to the suburbs for flat blocks.

A Local Government department inquiry in City Hall held from 23 April 1942, considered objections to eight preliminary purchase orders by the Corporation for sites near the scene of the North Strand bombing. Representing the Corporation, Ignatius Rice said that even before the bombing, many of the premises were

already unfit for human habitation, while an extensive
section had already been scheduled for clearance and
rehousing. The Neutrality (War Damage to Property)
Act enabled the Corporation to consider acquiring and
clearing the area earlier than planned. The Corporation
had already rehoused 242 families in Cabra, Crumlin and
other parts. Of the 542 families living in the area before
the bombing, 224 remained; of sixty-two local shops,
seventeen were destroyed.

A plan prepared by Simms for the 18-acre site would
provide 519 dwellings or, alternatively, 493 dwellings and
thirty-six shops, along with a children's playground and an
industrial zone in the south-eastern section, at a total cost
of around £400,000. Two further sites might be developed
as extensions to existing public and semi-public properties. Since any work on the site was unlikely in the next
five years, existing tenants could remain in their dwellings or shops. Michael O'Brien, the Corporation's acting
town-planning officer, said that, generally speaking, all the
properties had been damaged as a result of the bombing.
One objection came from the Great Southern Railways
Company, which was looking for an alternative site within
a reasonable distance of the docks to accommodate its
horse-drawn vehicles, then kept at Empress Place.

On the final day of the inquiry, Simms said that he
wished to clear up the matter of the ten unused shops in
Townsend Street, which a Mr Munden had claimed were
empty at an annual loss of £1,500 to ratepayers. Because

the shops were only completed during the present emergency, they were being used as community kitchens and for other ARP services, as well as for the storage of mobile canteens.

While the methods used were occasionally questionable, reconditioning existing houses in the city centre was proving considerably cheaper than building flat blocks in the same areas. An inquiry of November 1942 established that work was completed on 287 dwellings and continuing on a further 237; a total of 830 reconditioned dwellings was envisaged at a cost of £1.35 million. Upper Sean McDermott Street, Marlborough Street, Waterford Street and Lower Gardiner Street were all earmarked for reconditioning, with 357 families living in the area. A flats scheme of two- and three-room units and a kitchenette would have accommodated only 174 families. Despite the reconditioning work, the area around Gardiner Street continued its downward spiral until the 1980s.

ARP exercises resumed in January 1943, including spectacular rescues, bomb explosions ('maroons'), showers of incendiaries, simulated fire outbreaks and stretcher-bearing exercises involving firemen, ARP wardens and a hundred members of the rescue and demolition section marshalled by Simms as the chief rescue officer. One of its notable exploits was lowering a 'casualty' on a stretcher from the roof of a building in Upper O'Connell Street, using a jib or derrick. In Lower Dominick Street,

several 'rescues' were undertaken from a house supposedly on fire after an explosion. Other manoeuvres took
place at Jervis Street Hospital, recreating a possible situation where a shower of incendiaries partly wrecked the
building, and in Abbey Street, where a 'cratered' road was
simulated with 'victims' buried in the debris.

On the second anniversary of the North Strand
bombing on 31 May 1943, Simms was on the saluting
platform for the ARP and North Strand civil defence
parade on the grounds of the Central Model School,
Marlborough Street. In that same year, Simms was
elected a fellow of the RIBA, proposed by John Joseph
Robinson and seconded by Patrick Abercrombie and
Frederick George Hicks.

Despite the Emergency and its aftermath, building
continued in Ballyfermot in 1941 and later in 1948 and
1949; in Cabra West from 1940 to 1946; in Crumlin
until 1944, in Donnycarney from 1947, and in Finglas
from the early 1950s. The thinning-out of the city continued during the war years and after the devastation
caused by the North Strand bombings, it seemed like a
sensible move.

A full review of the Corporation's plans in 1944
showed 8,257 dwellings built, which was some way
short of the 12,000 target. Only 2,480 houses were built
in 1943 and 1944. Building supplies were erratic and
tradesmen scarce because so many had left the country
for Britain where higher wages were on offer. Projects at

Newmarket, Donore Avenue, Rialto and Donnycarney were stalled and it would take years to get the momentum going again. Plans for Constitution Hill and Whitefriar Street were cancelled for town-planning reasons; in the case of Whitefriar Street, a proposed road development was the cause. In 1944, with some 18,000 families in need of housing, the Corporation revised its plans. The target for the five years from 1944 was 7,450 houses in Cabra West, Donnycarney, Rialto, Donore Avenue, plus the Crumlin area around Rutland Avenue and unbuilt land to the north and south of the district, as well as further developments in Ballyfermot around Sarsfield Road, and at the existing schemes at Collins Avenue, Ellenfield and Larkhill.

Although the target of 1,490 houses a year looked impressive, it was nowhere near the 3,700 houses a year advocated by the 1939–43 Housing Inquiry. The inquiry had suggested that 1,200 units be built by outside agencies – this left a gap of about 1,000 per year between what the Corporation felt was possible and what the inquiry reckoned was necessary.

One possible solution again floated was direct building by the Corporation. It was hardly a novel idea since Associated Properties, the public utility society, had been building its own houses for a decade. Yet those in charge were reluctant to take that approach. Both the Corporation and Associated Properties believed that greater state support was needed to meet the proposed housing targets. Patrick Hernon noted that state support for housing had continued to fall below costs. When the subsidy scale was established in 1932, the maximum housing costs that could be supported was £500, which was an adequate sum when the 'all-in' building cost was £560 for a flat and £430 for a cottage. By 1945, building a cottage was almost double the cost at £850.

Little had changed in public policy since the 1930s, with the Corporation still overwhelmed by the magnitude of the housing crisis. Although it had built on a huge scale and changed the face of the city, fundamental problems persisted. With no overall plan, the Minister for Local Government and the Corporation continued to deal piecemeal with each housing crisis as it arose. Yet as Manning Robertson had noted in his 1944 *Handbook of National Planning and Reconstruction*, Dublin Corporation alone had produced a 'sketch' plan as required under the 1934 town-planning legislation. Three other boroughs and a few county councils had taken provisional steps, but by and large, the Act's regional provisions had been an abject failure.

At national level, politicians were attempting to strike a balance between urban and rural development, believing that improved standards of life in more remote areas would help stem the flight from the land and ease the pressure on Dublin housing. In the early 1940s a view prevailed that houses with a garden in the suburbs could keep a family well fed, and, in some fringe areas, housebuilding was postponed because of the need to maintain allotments and garden farming at a time when food was short.

Attracting attention at the time was Noel Moffett, an innovative architect with an experimental approach to housing, who organised a National Planning Exhibition at the Mansion House in 1944. Like Simms, Moffett had studied in Liverpool under Charles Reilly and later mixed with other younger modernist architects like Michael Scott. A lively character, he had joined Dublin Corporation in 1941 before setting up his own practice in 1944 and becoming a pioneer of modern architecture, building innovative modernist houses in Portmarnock and a scheme of local-authority housing for Dundalk Urban District Council. After he moved to London, high-density public housing became a mainstay of his practice.

For his part, Simms was vastly overworked. His correspondence about the Captain's Lane development in Crumlin began in October 1944 with a request that the city manager pursue a compulsory purchase order for a playground site. It would be designed by Simms and built as a 'Relief Labour Scheme'. As well as planning the first phase of 802 houses, he set aside five acres for a convent and schools and over an acre for eight shops and a cinema.

By February 1945 Simms was working on the second section of the scheme, with 589 houses planned, as well as a community centre, an alternative site for the GAA, a re-shaped site for Carlisle Athletics Club, a church site, two schools (boys and girls), a dispensary, a library and an industrial site. 'The whole scheme has been planned as a self-contained neighbourhood unit and not as a housing extension to the two previous Crumlin schemes though, of course, the demarcation of one scheme with another cannot be made too hard and fast,' Simms told a later inquiry.

Every element of the design involved meetings and negotiations. Forcing several alterations to the plans were John Charles McQuaid, who was the Catholic Archbishop of Dublin, and the Corporation's own town planning department. It was exhausting and often frustrating work, requiring considerable diplomatic as well as architectural skills.

9

The Final Projects 1945–8

By the time the Second World War ended on 2 September 1945 Ireland had built up a large sterling balance, allowing the government to embark on an ambitious £5 million development programme. Seán Lemass' White Paper on 'The Post-War Building Programme' predicted that housing would constitute the nation's biggest building and economic project, taking up over half of the building budget. Public building highlights included the completion of a hydroelectric scheme on the River Liffey and the foundation of CIE, with Michael Scott commissioned to design a bus depot for Donnybrook and Ove Arup – the British company newly arrived in Ireland – employed as engineer for the project. Between 1946 and 1953, Scott would design and oversee the building of Busáras at Store Street, at the time seen as almost shockingly innovative in design.

Steel shortages after the war spurred experiments in concrete, which became increasingly used for factory, school and swimming-pool roofs. Building costs had increased since the war began and it now took over £1,000 to recondition a city-centre flat in Dublin, double the figure of four years earlier. Labour was not cheap and land had risen in price. Pre-war, an acre of land in Crumlin had cost £200; this figure soared to £1,000 by 1945.

At the end of June 1945 and after twenty-three years in the position, Horace O'Rourke had retired as city architect. He was not officially replaced for some years, although Conor McGinley, a 1916 veteran and assistant city architect since 1922, took over as acting city architect and was officially appointed to the role in 1947.

In a response to the 1939–40 housing inquiry report in December 1945, the city engineer Noel Taylor and the Town Planning Office made it clear that the Corporation's policy of providing large areas of single-class housing in areas such as Cabra and Crumlin would not be repeated. Future developments would have a mix of tenants, as had happened on Collins Avenue and Larkhill where a number of public utility societies took up the Corporation's offer of sites. On the south side of the city, the middle-class structure of housing developments was already established, which meant that encouraging a social mix would prove tricky. With public housing, the plan was to subsidise half the houses in a project and to recoup some of the cost by selling other houses and looking for a full economic rent in the remainder. The Corporation would continue to work closely with public utility companies such as Associated Properties, which had become by some way the largest such company.

Following the initial optimism of the post-Second World War era came an unsettled period in Irish politics with successive changes of government. Dublin was still a city of stark contrasts – filthy streets and neglected tenement buildings existed only a short walk away from a rebuilt and bustling O'Connell Street.

In January 1946, Simms and Joseph Sherwin of the Housing Department along with Michael O'Brien, the town planning officer, took two visiting British MPs on an inspection tour of public housing schemes. The MPs duly expressed their admiration not only for the houses, but for churches, schools and other facilities provided.

In April Michael O'Brien told an inquiry into a compulsory purchase of a site between Philipsburgh Avenue, Fairview, and Grace Park Road in Drumcondra, that the Corporation would need 46,000 new houses and at least 3,000 additional acres of land to complete its housing programme.

Patrick Hernon said that space at the proposed site would be reserved for six residential shops on Philipsburgh Avenue, a two-acre children's play park and two small open spaces. After representations from the trustees of St Vincent's Mental Home, the Corporation had agreed to exclude from their plans 13 acres belonging to the home. For his part, Simms explained that a strip of ground was needed to allow the Corporation widen Philipsburgh Avenue and to erect fourteen more houses. One of the objections to the scheme came from St Joseph's Male Blind Asylum, Drumcondra. Under the proposed plan, they would lose close to 4 acres of ground they used as a vegetable garden.

In early October 1946 Simms and Patrick Hernon travelled to Kingscourt in County Cavan for the opening of the Gyptex factory, which supplied the Corporation with plasterboard. Only 563 houses were built by the Corporation in 1946. Circumstances were working against a promised post-war revival, with the non-stop rain of 1946 resulting in bread rationing from January 1947. A bitterly cold winter followed with not enough coal available before the Anglo-Irish trade agreement of November 1947 ensured a better supply. Trams were cancelled and factories closed down. A Department of Social Welfare, with James Ryan its first minister, was established in January 1947, taking over many functions of the Department of Local Government.

With Fianna Fáil insisting that building houses for renting to workers had top priority, construction in 1947 was up 46 per cent on 1946 despite the erratic supply of materials. In an effort to curtail speculative development, priority was given to local authorities and to individuals building houses for themselves, which would attract subsidies under the Housing Acts. Of the 4,399 houses built across the country in 1947, 37.4 per cent were built by local authorities. The situation was still dire. In October 1947 came a compulsory purchase order for houses on Rutland Street off Summerhill, some of them in danger of collapse.

Architecture as a profession was fighting its corner and, as early as 1945, Gerald McNicholl of the RIAI had written to the Department of Local Government emphasising the role that architects could play in the design of public housing as they did in Europe and Great Britain. A dispute over fees scuppered a competition proposed by the department for three representative schemes (urban, rural and village) in January 1948. While Irish architects were happy to voice their criticism of Corporation housing, they failed to come up with an alternative plan, although Noel Moffett did suggest that flat blocks should be doubled in size to eight storeys in order to make them more efficient.

In 1947, with the rapid rise of Clann na Poblachta threatening the position of Fianna Fáil, Éamon de Valera introduced an Act that increased the size of the Dáil from 138 to 147 members and the number of three-seat constituencies from 15 to 22. He then called an election for 4 February 1948. Despite his machinations, Fianna Fáil still lost out to a combination of Fine Gael, Clann na Poblachta, Labour, Clann na Talmhan, the National Labour Party and a number of independents. These would make up the country's first inter-party government, elected on pledges to improve housing and public health. John A. Costello of Fine Gael was elected as Taoiseach and William Norton of Labour as Tánaiste and Minister for Social Welfare.

By 1948 the Corporation's Town Planning and Housing Committee, with thirty-five members, was increasingly ineffectual and a Housing Consultative Council was formed to mastermind the renewed housing push. T.C. O'Mahoney, the former Limerick city manager, who was appointed as the city's first housing director, made it clear that the Corporation intended acquiring every possible site in the city that could be used for building flats. On the fringes of the city, more sites were developed and a five-room plan was added to the list of appropriate designs.

In the council's 1948 report, signed by O'Mahoney, a labour shortage was blamed for the failure to meet post-war housing targets, with the workforce disorganised and malnourished; the war and mass emigration to England and Scotland had taken their toll. In 1938, 163 bricklayers were available for work in the city; by 1944, that number had fallen to 69. Over the same period, the number of carpenters had dropped from 562 to 202; of plumbers from 60 to 13, while plasterers were down from 323 to 73.

The cost of constructing a 'cottage' was now £1,200, while a flat cost much more at £1,800. Some 1,513 dwellings were near completion in newly developed estates at Donnycarney and Ballyfermot.

Fianna Fáil's 1948 White Paper 'Housing – a Review of Past Operations and Immediate Requirements' had highlighted the need for a large-scale housing programme to eradicate existing slums and eliminate overcrowding. The White Paper proposed constructing 100,000 houses within ten years, with 60,000 to be provided by local authorities and 40,000 by private builders.

Launching the first post-war housing drive was the Housing (Amendment) Act of 1948, which increased the grant for private houses to £275 and introduced regulations for the management and letting of local-authority houses. Fianna Fáil's White Paper, along with the 1948 Act, was largely adopted by the incoming administration, with the Department of Local Government transformed into a virtual Department of Housing under the brief leadership of the minister, Timothy J. Murphy of the Labour Party, who would die suddenly in April 1949. He was replaced by Michael Keyes, also Labour.

During 1948, 2,778 dwellings were completed, with a further 1,151 under construction. Underway were housing schemes in Donnycarney and at Sarsfield Road in Ballyfermot as well as the revived flat developments. Planned for Finglas was a major new scheme for 4,000 houses at Cardiff Lane. Newlyweds and elderly people were given priority on the housing list, followed by families with a member suffering from tuberculosis, and

163

persons living in unfit and overcrowded housing. Strict licensing of building work was introduced, with state-aided housing initially afforded priority, though this move was later dropped.

Around the same time, the Australian Raymond McGrath was appointed principal architect at the OPW, having worked as a senior architect in the office since 1940. He would continue in the post until 1968. Although he would work on restoring Dublin Castle and other landmark public buildings, McGrath was a modernist who dreamed of creating a pristine, modern city with wide, car-friendly streets.

After T.C. O'Mahoney and a team of Corporation officials, including Simms, visited London and Glasgow, the new housing programme was instigated with a target of building 30,000 dwellings in Dublin over a ten-year period. Of these, 5,000 were designated as flats. Of the 3,000 units to be built per year, a thousand would be prefabricated in aluminium, timber or steel. The sum of £39 million was to be raised to cover state-aided loans.

Although cottages and reconditioning clearly dominated the Corporation's housing plans, Simms was taking another look at the three large-scale schemes he had begun planning in the early 1940s: Fatima Mansions and St Teresa's Gardens on the fringes of the city and the Newfoundland Street and Sheriff Street scheme in the docks area. With these schemes, on more generous public spaces, Simms was attempting to create self-contained urban communities, influenced by the German cost-effective *Neue Sachlichkeit* ('New Objectivity') formula from the 1920s, which emphasised providing healthy living conditions for urban dwellers. Flat complexes in the *Zeilenbau* ('row houses') style were grouped carefully on a site and orientated to allow for maximum sunlight and ventilation, as advocated by Gropius and the Bauhaus.

Simms retained the low-rise deck-access approach typical of his earlier work, with all flats having a front door onto an outdoor corridor or 'deck' accessed by an exterior stair block. Ironically, the deck access used in most Simms schemes proved more innovative than his critics Moffett and Scott allowed. In 1951 Alison and Peter Smithson's scheme for the Golden Lane estate in London proposed 'streets in the sky' for the first time in the UK, mixing elements of Le Corbusier's *Unité d'Habitation* internal streets and the traditional British working-class street with its front doors to each dwelling. Although the design was not realised, it was used later in Sheffield's Park Hill, built between 1957 and 1961, and became increasingly popular in the 1960s.

Clearly, these new European-influenced urban schemes were no longer the four-storey blocks built in sympathy with existing streets typical of the pre-war years. Unfortunately, placing 'streets' in the air and cutting off residents from direct access to the streets would prove a social and human disaster.

When the supply of building materials returned to normal, work resumed on the flats at Rialto and Donore Avenue and on the second phase of the Newfoundland Street/Sheriff Street scheme, where 576 flats were envisaged along with thirty-two shops. After the government had given its approval in 1938, tenants were moved out and the area cleared. By 1942, close to 150 flats were complete, although progress was slow due to shortages, and work virtually came to a standstill in 1944. After building finally resumed in 1948, Simms signed off on the contracts, although Donald Tyndall was the supervisory architect. Tyndall had worked in the housing architect's office from around 1933 to 1937 and later on public projects in Cavan before enlisting in the Royal Engineers Corps as an officer during the Second World War. On his return to Dublin, he set up his own practice, often working for local authorities.

True to the modernist ethos, the blocks of Newfoundland Street/Sheriff Street scheme were arranged on staggered lines and situated in a triangle bounded by the docks, the canal and the railway, with Simms writing, 'the blocks run from North to South which is the accepted ideal'. They would house about 560 families and 2,500 children; only in 1952 were the eighteen four-storey flat blocks completed. Called St Laurence's Mansions, St Brigid's Gardens and Phil Shanahan House, the entire scheme was demolished in the 1980s and replaced by seven three-storey blocks. These blocks in their turn were later demolished.

In the case of Fatima Mansions, the scheme of fifteen four-storey blocks mixing perimeter and *Zeilenbau* layouts was located on a site linking Reuben Street and St Anthony's Road, both off the South Circular Road. Constructed on a curving road with junctions, the large blocks appeared cramped and awkward. Postwar shortages meant the use of brick was limited to the ground-floor level and to the towers at the end of each block; the detail shows a lack of refinement untypical of Simms or of his office. Ultimately, Fatima Mansions was the most disappointing of Simms' major schemes and, as with Sheriff Street, question marks remain over his involvement. Crampton's, the contractors, maintained that he never once visited the site.

More successful was the St Teresa's Gardens scheme off Donore Avenue where Simms was using a *Zeilenbau* arrangement exactly as recommended. At the entrance were four blocks marked by curved towers and containing shops; behind them, ten identical four-storey blocks were aligned. The original drawings for St Teresa's Gardens from 1940 had featured pitched roofs and detailed stairwells, but these proved too expensive. A shortage of angle irons meant architectural balconies and the brick 'soldier' course over the window openings were also abandoned. The spaces between the blocks proved a problem; because they were neither courtyard nor garden, they became a confused no-man's land. The design and layout of the 346-flat complex gave rise to antisocial behaviour and all but two of the original flat blocks were torn down in 2016.

Prefabrication was the new by-word in housing circles and steel house prototypes were produced after the war by a number of companies, including Orlit in Ireland. In 1947 the Corporation set up a prefabrication committee, which lasted only a few months. Prefabrication was proving expensive and because by-laws ruled that walls should be built in stone, concrete or brick with a minimum 9-inch thickness, timber or cavity walls were banned. Simms had always objected to prefabricating houses as an expensive and poor-quality solution to the housing problem.

Reviewing progress in 1948, the Corporation noted the delays in the system, despite some improvements. Once tenders were agreed, the Corporation moved swiftly to place contracts and the supply chain was improving, although skilled tradesmen were still in short supply. Building techniques for emergency housing developed in Britain during the war were discussed. The Dublin Household Consultative Council, drawn from various councils, along with state officials, viewed various projects and again considered using prefabs made from pre-cast concrete and galvanised steel with bitumen felt for the roof. Although as yet these could not compete with brick-built housing either in terms of cost or quality, they were not ruled out.

It was all too much for Simms, who had already suffered one nervous collapse from overwork early in his career.

On Monday, 27 September 1948, two months before his fiftieth birthday, he drove his car to Dún Laoghaire, a bottle of whiskey in his pocket. Sometime later that evening, he threw himself in front of a train near Coal Quay bridge. The following morning he was found on the tracks, barely alive and with one arm amputated. He died later that day at nearby St Michael's Hospital. A handwritten note was found in his pocket, which read: 'I cannot stand it any longer, my brain is too tired to work any more. It has not had a rest for 20 years except when I am in heavy sleep. It is always on the go like a dynamo and still the work is being piled on to me.' 'No flowers, prayers instead' said the death notice.

Following an inquest on 30 September, Simms was buried in Deansgrange cemetery after a funeral in St John the Baptist Church, Blackrock, on Friday 1 October. On 4 October Dublin Corporation passed a vote of sympathy to his wife and family, with Patrick Hernon, the city manager, leading numerous tributes. He died intestate. His widow Eileen, who was ten years younger than Simms, would remarry and later gave birth to a daughter, Pauline Williams. Eileen died in 1978 and, like her first husband, is buried in Deansgrange cemetery.

Simms had been the guiding light of the slum–clearance programme of the 1930s and the widespread appreciation of his work was clearly evident in the tributes paid to him. 'His flat blocks remain elegant architectural documents of an intense vision and commitment in Irish public life of the 1930s to banish the evil of slum over-crowding forever,' said one.

His friend Ernest Taylor, the city surveyor, paid tribute to Simms in an obituary published in the *Irish Builder*.

> Behind a quiet and unassuming manner there lurked a forceful personality; and Mr Simms could uphold his point of view with a vigour that sometimes surprised those who did not know him well. By sheer hard work and conscientious devotion to duty, he has made a personal contribution towards the solution of Dublin's housing problem, probably unequalled by anyone in our time. It is not given to many of us to achieve so much in the space of a short lifetime for the benefit of our fellow men.

Housing dominated local government in the 1930's and again from the 1950s to the 60s, with decisions taken largely by accountants rather than by architects. Desmond FitzGerald, president of the Architectural Association of Ireland in 1948, had worried that if the public did not take an interest in architecture 'it will be produced in such a rarefied atmosphere that it will gasp for breath amidst subtleties of interest only to architects themselves'. Unfortunately, it was at this point that Dublin Corporation lost Simms, its most dynamic and conscientious architect.

In December 1948, three months after the death of Simms, the inter-party government ended all Ireland's remaining political links with the United Kingdom. The Irish Free State officially became the Republic of Ireland on Easter Monday, 18 April 1949, the thirty-third anniversary of the 1916 Easter Rising.

Housing would remain the principal preoccupation of the Department of Local Government until the late 1950s. In 1949/50, local authorities built 5,299 houses, compared to 619 in the period 1946/7. The number of houses built and reconstructed by private individuals and public utility companies rose from 1,146 in 1946/7 to 3,916 in 1949–50. Under the 1948 Act, Associated Properties could claim £240 per house for its enormous Wadelai development off Ballymun Road. Construction began in the late 1940s and, as was usual with Associated Properties, the design of the houses was close to the Corporation's own template. On completion, Wadelai provided homes for several hundred families.

It was hoped that the investment in housing would provide jobs and encourage a return of skilled labourers from the building sites of Britain to Ireland. Sadly, in the years to come, less attention was paid to good design and appropriate locations. Large swathes of Georgian Dublin were demolished and replaced by bland and poorly designed office blocks, while medieval streets were obliterated to make more room for the ubiquitous motor car. Dublin as a city was losing its heart and its distinctive character.

10

What Followed Simms

From 1949 to 1957 and into the 1960s Ireland experienced a deep depression, which provoked a return of mass emigration. Among those leaving the country were architects, carpenters, electricians, plasterers and skilled bricklayers. Governments changed frequently. Fianna Fáil was back in power from 1951 to 1954 after three years of the inter-party government. The inter-party government returned from 1954 to 1957 after which Fianna Fáil began a sixteen-year reign lasting until 1973.

Simms' name cropped up in December 1950 when a five-year-old action against the Dublin Corporation concerning a contract for building flat blocks in the Cook Street housing area was finally settled. In March 1934 a tender from Messrs Meagher & Hayes for building thirteen blocks of flats to contain 312 dwellings at a cost of £154,771 was accepted by the Corporation. The builders later argued that a certificate of Simms' dated 15 June 1940, which stated that the balance due was £1,857 5s 5d, was not a true final certificate. Dublin Corporation agreed to pay £2,257 5s 5d plus costs.

In 1949 a lavish pamphlet was circulated by Dublin Corporation in an attempt to lure emigrant labourers back to Ireland from the building sites of Great Britain, with the slogan 'Ireland Is Building'. It outlined plans for building 3,219 dwellings immediately and a further 15,000, along with schools and churches, over ten years, guaranteeing plenty of work. Politicians at the time believed that citizens who owned their own houses would have a greater stake in the country; that was certainly the view of the Taoiseach John Costello in 1950.

Yet in Continental Europe, a majority of city-dwellers rented their homes and Le Corbusier's hugely influential *Unité d'Habitation* built in Marseilles from 1947 to 1952 was designed to allow city-based families to live independently in one large and publicly-owned building. In Ireland, renting a privately-owned flat was regarded as a temporary measure while working towards the deposit for a house; renting a publicly-owned flat was only an option for the desperate. Not helping was the Catholic Church's opposition to the quasi-communal life of the flat block, led by the Dublin Archbishop John Charles McQuaid, who continued to make frequent phone calls to the Housing Department.

Even the newspapers joined in, with the conservative *Irish Times* coming up with five arguments against flat living. Apart from being more expensive to build, flats wasted space, were dangerous to young life and were unhealthy. Most crucially, they did not satisfy the need in every Irish man and woman for a 'home of their own'. As far as the newspaper's middle-class owners were concerned, domestic bliss for the working classes lay in rows of identikit terraced homes built on the fringes of the city.

Serious social problems could and did arise in flat blocks and in public housing generally, especially when the more reliable tenants availed of government initiatives to allow them buy their own houses. With the loss of these solid citizens, housing estates and flat blocks became more prone to vandalism, joyriding, drug abuse and gang warfare, especially after many large industries that would have hired unskilled workers closed down in the 1970s. When recession hit, public – as well as private – income was affected, and local authorities found that they could no longer afford to service and maintain their housing schemes.

After the death of Herbert Simms came a house-building frenzy that would shape the city forever. Village communities on the fringe of the city were swallowed up and green fields disappeared under concrete. With the Housing (Amendment) Act of 1950, new grant-aided houses became eligible for rates remission, which made buying a home more affordable.

Expenditure on housing provision rose dramatically during the 1950s. In the sixteen years from April 1948, about 137,000 dwellings were built with state aid, of which 74,000 were provided by private enterprise compared to 63,000 by local authorities. Capital expenditure on housing between 1948 and 1964 was estimated at £225 million, with state aid and local authorities contributing £192 million. The balance – less than 15 per cent of total capital – was provided by banks, building societies, assurance companies and savings.

Post-war European governments had adopted the Keynesian economic model of increasing state intervention to control the cycle of boom and bust, which was seen as the root cause of political extremism. In Ireland, the government believed that every £1.5 million spent on housing grants generated a further £10 million in private expenditure. Its immediate plans included building 9,000 houses spread between schemes in Finglas, Sarsfield Road in Ballyfermot and Dundrum. Of those, 3,000 would be built using alternative construction methods. In 1949 construction of over 500 houses began at Captain's Avenue in Crumlin using the Orlit system. Problems caused by the thin walls, shoddy plastering, no flue lines and a lack of ventilation space under the ground floor quickly became apparent. It was clear that the system was more complicated and less adaptable than classic building methods, although concrete blocks were soon overtaking the traditional masonry and brick systems for load-bearing walls.

By 1951 Dublin's population had risen to 569,000, which was one-fifth of the Irish population. Despite a government decentralisation policy promoted since 1931, power was not truly devolved to local authorities; the administration of health, social welfare and education was still centralised. For public resources, such as electricity and transport, a form of government unique to Ireland was created: the state-sponsored body. Public employment at local level shrank.

A half-baked decentralisation policy, conservative social thinking influenced by the Catholic Church, the cost of inner-city sites and an anti-urban bias both in government and the media had led to the growth of public housing on the fringes of the city. Yet Irish architects were hardly unaware of the large-scale flat-block schemes, which were helping rebuild the battered cities of post-war Europe.

At yet another housing enquiry held in May 1951, T.C. O'Mahoney outlined future plans for flat blocks and explained how they could be used to regenerate the inner city. Small-scale schemes were planned for tenement black spots, among them Alfie Byrne House near Mountjoy Square, Leo Fitzgerald House near Westland Row and James Larkin House on the site of the North Strand bombings.

In the Dublin Development Plan of 1953, the Corporation listed sixty sites for tenement clearance, making explicit its intention to return to building flat blocks at the core of the city and in the inner suburbs. By November 1956, work had begun on thirty sites, with a total of 6,000 flats the target. Many of them were small in scale, such as the 22-unit block on Ballygall Road and a 24-unit block at Collins Place, Finglas, both built in 1953, and similar blocks at Bluebell Road and Huband Road close by. Other flat blocks of varying size were built in areas such as Drimnagh, Dolphin's Barn, Ringsend, Rathmines Avenue and Whitefriar Street.

The post of housing architect remained unfilled, with RIAI members arguing that an annual salary of £1,050 rising to £1,350 was too low considering the responsibilities and stresses of a job that included managing an annual budget of £3 million. Only in 1956 did Dún Laoghaire Borough Corporation architect Dáithi Hanly take up the position. Hanly had overseen a major housing scheme consisting of 1,000 houses at Sallynoggin and, with the support of T.C. O'Mahoney, he came up with designs for four- and five-storey blocks of flats using standardised components, which helped reduce the cost of the buildings and were easier to maintain.

Probably the finest of the post-Simms flat schemes was Leo Fitzgerald House, designed by Charles McNamara and finally completed in 1958; it was the first flat complex to be built in the south-east inner city since the 1930s. Plans for the scheme at Hogan Place and Erne Street, first suggested in 1951, were delayed because of problems acquiring a valuable site. With Crampton's the builders, this 48-unit block proved expensive because of the high initial expenditures – the entire scheme cost £169,500. Instead of the decks or galleries with shared external stairways typical of the Simms schemes, Hogan Place used a more costly walk-up block and four stairways. A four-roomed flat cost £3,689 to build and Patrick 'Pa' O'Donnell, the Minister for Local Government from 1954 to 1957, initially refused to sanction the scheme.

James Larkin House at the North Strand, also designed by McNamara, consisted of three four-storey walk-up slab blocks, each with thirty-six units. It adapted Simms' designs, providing more practical and private open spaces where children could play safely. Little is known of McNamara, the acting housing architect; his father was an English plumber and he lived at 12 Donore Road. He had begun working as Simms' assistant and became deputy housing architect in 1939. Also on his team was Noel McGovern, who had been appointed to the Housing and City Architects department in 1948. Around 1946 the site between Grenville and Hill streets was planned as a terrace of reconditioned Georgian houses. Based on Noel McGovern's original drawings, it changed into a scheme of two five-storey perimeter blocks enclosing a quiet courtyard with modernist touches, called Alfie Byrne House. On the fourth and fifth storeys were duplex units spanning two storeys, which meant that fewer access decks were needed.

Residents and their needs took priority at another Charles McNamara scheme. Work on the Hardwicke Street flat blocks, named after Rory O'Connor and Dermot O'Dwyer, began in 1953, and was completed in 1957. These flat blocks, with rear deck access, provided 210 units in two four-storey blocks, curved to make an attractive crescent facing the neoclassical St George's Church, which dates back to 1813. Both schemes were traditionally built with load-bearing concrete block walls and reinforced concrete floors.

Anxious to try out new designs, McNamara had visited cities in England to study the latest flat developments. He came up with a new standard plan, with the first example built at Dolphin's Barn, which was criticised as being too expensive. By 1958, when Leo Fitzgerald House was complete, Dáithi Hanly and T.C. O'Mahoney were evolving a maisonette plan, which saw a return to the Simms-style deck template, although it added a free-standing external stairwell that was cheaper to construct.

At O'Devaney Gardens, built on 12 acres of cattle-grazing land off the North Circular Road in an Edwardian neighbourhood, the fourteen four-storey blocks were organised *Zeilenbau*-style in rows with deck access. The scheme, completed in 1955, was among those designed to house former residents of Dominick Street after that area was 'cleansed', as well as the displaced residents of Fairview and North Strand after the 1954 floods. Builders were McInerney, who also built the Bluebell, Hardwicke

Street and Dolphin House schemes, at an average cost of £2,238 for a five-roomed flat. That compared to £1,554 for a five-roomed house in Milltown.

Dolphin House on the Grand Canal in Rialto, providing 392 units, was completed in 1957 and partly renovated by 2018, with two of the blocks demolished to make way for the ambitious new design for the entire site. Block flats may have become synonymous with poverty and social problems, yet the best of them have stood the test of time.

So-called 'luxury flats' first appeared in Dublin in 1954 when the Mespil Road flats were constructed on a five-acre site at Sussex Road. Initially, the development, designed by W.J. Convery, consisted of eight four-storey flat-roofed blocks built in brick. Others followed in 1958 and 1967 when a seven-storey block containing fifty-six luxury flats was built. The final block, Elm House, was completed in 1972. In total, the estate provided 299 units. Amenities included a swimming pool.

For the re-developed Dominick Street in 1958, Desmond FitzGerald, as the consultant engineer, approved a draft proposal for a nine-storey tower. O'Mahoney objected, preferring traditionally built five-storey maisonette blocks, which stacked a pair of duplexes above a ground-floor flat. So began the era of the 'butterfly' or 'gull-winged' flat block, usually with a free-standing circular stair tower bridging the blocks at two levels. Between 1958 and 1975, about thirty-five of these maisonette schemes were built in Dublin, overseen by Dáithí Hanly. With blunt gable ends often facing the street, as at Kevin Street, these buildings made no attempt to blend into the existing streetscape.

In 1959, when the positions of housing architect and city architect were amalgamated, Hanly became Dublin city architect, responsible for all housing and civic architecture. More emphasis was placed on building flats. The target for 1954 had been 1,648 suburban houses to 853 central city dwellings and in 1955, 1,898 suburban houses to 588 flats. In 1956, 1,045 flats and 1,350 suburban houses were built.

By the mid-1950s the Corporation was housing around 170,000 tenants and in 1959, T.C. O'Mahoney estimated that about 40 per cent of the city's population was housed in the Corporation's 42,112 dwellings. The Corporation's borrowings at the time were £38.3 million under the Housing of the Working Classes Acts and almost £12 million under the Small Dwellings Acquisition Acts.

At last, flat schemes were grudgingly becoming acknowledged as a feature of urban life. Without people to live in them, streets die, schools and churches empty and local businesses fail. Ultimately, in a living city, the higher construction costs of a flat block were quickly paid off. Yet the Department of Local Government remained staunchly anti-urban. Even Alfie Byrne, back for a record tenth time as Lord Mayor from 1954 to 1955, supported road-widening plans that ploughed through the traditional streets and neighbourhoods of his native city.

Modernism took a firm hold of architecture in the 1950s, resulting in rectilinear buildings of steel, concrete and glass, with large windows, flat roofs, no excess decoration and open-plan interiors. Around the time of the Second World War, many of modernism's leading lights were to be found in the USA, which became a mecca for young Irish architects. Andy Devane studied with Frank Lloyd Wright in the late 1940s, Luan Cuffe worked with Gropius in the late 1940s and Kevin Roche went to the USA in the 1940s and never returned. Mies van der Rohe in Chicago with his 'almost nothing' functionalism and Louis Kahn in Pennsylvania were major influences when it came to corporate building.

Yet Britain, in particular post-war London housing, proved the greatest source of inspiration for the Corporation's architects. British architecture, influenced by Swedish design with a nod to Charles Rennie Mackintosh and the Arts and Crafts movement, remained more traditional and crafts-based.

The Housing (Amendment) Act 1958 increased grants for new houses and for reconstruction, as well as the installation of water and sewerage services and loans for reconstruction, repair or improvement to houses. Towards the end of the 1950s, the housing programme was largely seen as complete, with some believing that public housing was taking up too high a proportion of national capital expenditure.

At North Strand, the Charleville Mall maisonette scheme completed the reconstruction of the bombed-out site, with work on three five-storey flat blocks beginning in 1962 and the flats occupied by 1964. Later, the distinctive butterfly roof on the Corporation's flat blocks was replaced by a cheaper flat roof and mosaic panel. Maisonette blocks were phased out in the mid to late 1970s, when Corporation architects returned to Simms' design ideals aiming for greater integration into the surrounding streets and creating residential courtyards and playgrounds by 'hinging' blocks of flats.

By the early 1960s, the absence of any plan to create communities, the wisdom of subsidising private construction companies, and the official design plans for dwellings, were among the questions raised about the country's policy on urban development. Between 1936 and 1971, the population of Dublin living between the canals halved from 266,000 to 132,000, with traditional communities scattered to the suburbs. From 1946 to 1972, Dublin's office population grew steadily, reaching 90,000 in 1971 when almost half of all Irish office jobs were based in Dublin. With cars replacing bicycles and office blocks displacing homes, the city was increasingly abandoned after the working day, although pubs, theatres and cinemas kept the O'Connell Street and Grafton Street areas alive. Rathmines, Ringsend and Ballybough were now the inner suburbs.

Architects were arguing that Dublin's crumbling centre should be replaced by high-rise flat blocks and offices of between fifteen and twenty storeys. These would have lifts, roof gardens 'and all the modern conveniences', wrote Niall Montgomery in a widely-publicised paper called 'That'll All Have to Come Down' read to the Architectural Association in 1958. Typically, Raymond McGrath, architect with the OPW since 1940, who believed Dublin needed high-rise buildings and wide roads, described the attempt to preserve Georgian Dublin as 'a magnificent failure'.

A major influence on Irish architects at the time was Le Corbusier and the other high-minded utopians of British and European town planning who aimed to convert the chaos of older cities into 'machines for living in' with little regard for their history. In the case of dirty and dilapidated Dublin, admittedly built for a social elite, the Irish modernists and those that followed believed that nothing less than knocking it all down and starting anew would do. The arguments between traditionalists and modernists continued in Dublin Corporation. In 1965, when John J. Phelan, chairman of the Corporation's Housing Committee, was calling for flat blocks with eight or even nine storeys, T.C. O'Mahoney, the more traditionally-biased housing director, made quite clear his belief that anything taller than five storeys would reintroduce excessive density.

Dublin's housing crisis showed no sign of abating. In June 1963 three tenements on Bolton Street and Fenian

Street collapsed after a thunderstorm. Four people were killed. The Corporation evacuated 156 homes in a week and demolished a further 156 homes in eighteen months. Tenants were housed in former barracks, and other buildings and families were split up. Protests followed and a Dublin Housing Action Committee began squatting in empty buildings to oppose development plans. In 1965 the Department of the Environment estimated that 10,000 publicly-provided houses were urgently needed in Dublin. Two years later, 35,000 homes were considered the minimum needed to replace unfit dwellings, with a further 24,000 required to deal with overcrowding.

For a public increasingly concerned not just about housing but about the destruction of the country's building heritage, the breaking point came in April 1965 when the ESB demolished sixteen early nineteenth-century Georgian buildings at Fitzwilliam Street to make way for its head office. Earlier plans to demolish the Georgian terrace had been thwarted when the Second World War was declared in 1939.

Adding to the outrage, Fitzwilliam Street, once part of the longest stretch of Georgian architecture in the world, was destroyed by a supposedly responsible state-sponsored body. Sam Stephenson, the architect responsible, argued that Georgian houses were 'never intended to last more than a lifetime' and that 'they cannot be usefully preserved at all'. The lacklustre office blocks which replaced them were themselves demolished in late 2017. It was an era when historic eighteenth- and nineteenth-century buildings were wantonly replaced by undistinguished office blocks: the gloomy modernism of Mount Street Lower is the most egregious of many examples.

A revived Georgian Society and increased interest in Dublin's vernacular buildings were two direct results of Fitzwilliam Street's destruction. In the 'Battle of Hume Street' in 1969, a new generation of architectural students made their voices heard. Their protests fell on deaf ears. An unhealthy relationship had evolved between some politicians and certain developers, who had no interest in promoting a rational planning policy when it went against their own interests. The 1973 Kenny Report showed that the price of serviced land in the county of Dublin had jumped from £1,100 per acre in 1960 to £7,000 per acre in 1971.

Out of the desperate need for public housing came the hasty decision to build at Ballymun, supposedly inspired by Le Corbusier's 'towers in the park'. The architects were Arthur Swift and Partners, an English practice already responsible for some of Dublin's more contentious projects, including St Michael's Estate, Inchicore, built in 1969 (demolished) and the Fingal County Council office on O'Connell Street (demolished). Ballymun, completed in 1969, provided 3,021 dwellings in total, divided between the fifteen-storey point blocks, nineteen eight-storey deck-access spine blocks and ten four-storey walk-up blocks. All flats came with a bathroom and kitchen.

From the start, problems arose with regulating the heat in the flat blocks, while the lifts kept breaking down and general maintenance was poor. Little attention was paid to providing essential amenities such as shops and green spaces and, although a town centre was planned, it was delayed for years. In 1985 came the scheme to encourage public housing tenants to buy their own homes, which, since it did not cover flats, meant that anybody living in a Ballymun flat who wanted to buy had to move out to a house. With the area becoming a watchword for poor social planning, the Ballymun flats were demolished between 2005 and 2015.

Myles Wright's *The Dublin Region: Advisory Regional Plan and Final Report* published in 1967 had outlined a £1,000 million programme for the physical development of the region by 1985. Wright, a town-planning expert from the University of Liverpool, believed that the population of Dublin would have grown by about 280,000 before 1985 with a further 40,000 living in the general region. He recommended the development of 'new towns' with populations of between 60,000 and 100,000 at 'Western Towns' in Tallaght, Blanchardstown, Lucan and Clondalkin. In the outer region, Drogheda and the Newbridge-Kilcullen-Naas district would take priority, followed by Arklow and Navan. A grid-like road system around the city would take account of 'the accepted fact that the motor car is becoming everyone's mode of conveyance', in theory spreading the commuting traffic over new and existing roads.

Under the 1970 Dublin Development Plan, urban sprawl continued. With no consideration given to the provision of efficient public transport, commuters living not only in the outer reaches of County Dublin at Portmarnock, Malahide, Leixlip and Shankill but also in the neighbouring counties of Meath, Kildare and Wicklow had no choice but to use cars. Living in their native city is no longer an option for the majority of Dubliners.

A Fianna Fáil government under Charles Haughey made the populist decision in 1977 to abolish the domestic rates system, which financed local government. While the system was certainly in need of reform, once it ceased to exist, local councils became almost entirely dependent on central government for their funding and this fell far short of what was needed. Not only was the abolition of rates a blow to local democracy, it also resulted in higher rates of income tax and VAT.

In 1985 came the reform of Local Government (Reorganisation) Act, under which the greater Dublin area would be managed not by two but by four local councils. While it promised devolution, it did not solve the two fundamentally anti-democratic issues dating back to the Irish Free State's first government of 1922: the grip of central government on local politics and the councils' inability to raise their own funds.

From the late nineteenth century and for the early decades of the twentieth century, Dublin Corporation had a major role in providing housing for the most needy of its citizens. After Irish independence, over-centralised government created an administrative gridlock, with the specific needs of urban communities ignored. TDs, whose priority, in theory, is national issues, became all too dominant in the administration of what should be locally accessible public services. In France, the lowest tier of administration, the *commune*, headed by a mayor, can consist of as few as 300 citizens; in Ireland, the lowest tier of local administration consists of 36,000 citizens. In Germany, a multi-tiered system of sixteen *Länder* has responsibility for health, justice, education, policing and culture. The federal government sets policy, which is then administered by the *Länder*. In Switzerland, twenty-six cantons operate largely free from national interference; in Costa Rica, a country with a population only slightly lower than that of Ireland, local government is devolved to eighty-two cantons. Will Dubliners ever have that kind of say in the running of their city?

There is good news. Many of the Simms buildings remain intact. The Oliver Bond flats, built in 1936 at Usher's Quay beside the massive Guinness brewery, celebrated its 80th anniversary in 2016. Over the years, about 10,000 tenants encompassing three generations have passed through its 388 units. Chancery House is now a revered gem of Irish modernism, closely followed by Pearse House, Countess Markievicz House, Marrowbone Lane,

Ballybough House and Henrietta Street. Work has begun on updating many of the Simms buildings.

Helping greatly is a more positive approach to urban living. In the 1990s, urban renewal schemes began reversing a policy of hollowing out the inner city had begun in 1936. Key to this were the apartment blocks built by private developers for middle-class office workers, who wanted to live in the city centre, near their work and also to social activities. Dublin Corporation started building terraces of public housing in places such as City Quay and the North Wall which, although far from architectural gems, are in the spirit of the Simms flats and cottages and the 1960s maisonettes. Flats have returned, most notably at Railway Street near Herbert Simms' Liberty House, while St Mary's Mansions has undergone an extensive facelift; as has Dolphin House in Rialto.

Herbert Simms is the hero of this story. He never forgot the needs of Dublin's poorest citizens and, over more than sixteen years, took on small-minded accountants, interfering local councillors, grasping contractors and conservative religious leaders while building some 17,000 dwellings for those citizens. His graceful buildings have survived because they are sturdy and properly designed as well as beautiful. Like the Georgian terraces before them, they are an essential part of Dublin's story.

Let us cherish them.

Appendices

A. Flat Complexes 1932–50

AVONDALE HOUSE (1934-6)
In the inner city, Avondale House on North Cumberland Street, off Parnell Street, was a neat development of three blocks with pitched roofs and canted corners built around an entrance courtyard. It provided sixty-six flats and included a Penny Dinner hall.

BALLYBOUGH HOUSE (1936–9)
A total of six flat schemes were completed in 1939, providing 712 flats. Among them was Ballybough House at Poplar Row, which was outside the city's central area within the two canals. Tenders were invited in April 1936 for three blocks of 111 flats along with a pump house and retaining wall. It was hoped to house tenants from the Newfoundland Street area of docklands in the scheme,

at least until the long-delayed Sheriff Street scheme was completed. When finished, Ballybough House proved an exceptional example of early twentieth-century modernist architecture with its arched entrances, curved corners with windows and facades of mixed brickwork and render.

CHANCERY HOUSE (1934-5)

After St Michan's House, Simms' next completed scheme, built between 1934 and 1935 in just eight months, was the Amsterdam-influenced Chancery House in Charles Street, not far from St Michan's House, where the contractor was G. & T. Crampton. Because of the project, Mountrath Street, known as one of Dublin's shortest streets with only four tenement houses, disappeared entirely from the map. Of the twenty-seven units, sixteen were two-roomed and eleven three-roomed; the two-roomed flats were considered particularly suitable for older tenants. Rent was 1s 9d per room.

With its flat roof, overhanging eaves, rounded corners, projecting balconies and brick detail, this compact L-shaped three-storey block was quintessential Simms, highlighting his innovative use of simple materials and his attention to detail. Although small, the scheme was considered a masterclass in public housing, and boasts a beautiful small garden, complete with an elegant entrance arch and kiosk. A plaque commemorating Simms was later placed on the arch.

EMMET BUILDINGS (1936–8)

Emmet Buildings in Watling Street near the Guinness brewery were ready for occupation in 1938. Tenders were invited in December 1935, with G. & T. Crampton the contractors and fifty-five flats provided. Like Avondale House, Emmet Buildings consisted of three blocks around a courtyard with facades in render and red brick, and distinctive canted corners to the blocks.

FATIMA MANSIONS (1947–51)

How involved Simms was in the Fatima Mansions project is open to question; the foreman for the builders, G. & T. Crampton, claimed that Simms never once visited the site. Initial work on Fatima Mansions, linking Reuben Street and St Anthony's Road, both off the South Circular Road, had begun before the Second World War, with foundations laid in October 1940. Construction was held up due to the shortage of building materials and the first phase of fifteen four-storey blocks, with about twenty-seven flats in each unit, providing around 364 flats in all, was only completed in 1951, costing £1,576 per unit. With the 11-acre site flanked on one side by the Grand Canal and on another by Edwardian housing, the design was partly courtyard, partly row construction. Unlike smaller perimeter block schemes on narrow urban sites, it was awkwardly placed and out of synch with the immediate surroundings. Post-war shortages ordained wet-dashed elevations and the limited use of red brick, while Simms' usual attention to detail is absent. All in all, this was the most disappointing of Simms' major schemes, and by the 1980s it had become notorious for high levels of crime and drugs-related activity. It was demolished in the 2000s and replaced with a new housing scheme called Herberton.

GALTYMORE DRIVE (1943)
In Crumlin, at Galtymore Drive, a small block containing eight flats was completed in 1943.

GEORGE REYNOLDS HOUSE (1950)
In Irishtown, George Reynolds House at Oliver Plunkett Avenue was built by G. & T. Crampton for the Corporation and completed in 1950, providing seventy-six flats in a row of four blocks, with flat roofs, overhanging eaves and courtyard access from the rear.

HENRIETTA HOUSE (1935–9)
Henrietta House, off the Georgian Henrietta Street, was a compact scheme of forty-eight flats featuring curved corners in red brick, a flat overhanging roof, a yellow brick facade and imposing balconies. It was built as two blocks facing a central courtyard with access to the scheme through red-brick gate piers. Leading to the galleries at the rear were beautifully designed stair towers with a hint of the oriental. On the facade, the corner flats

had balconies in yellow stock brick with towers, projecting slightly but set in from the building's corners, which
curved to join an access deck at the rear. Simms used
simple materials, such as red brick, brown brick and a
variety of render finishes and textures, to provide visual
interest and contrast.

LIBERTY HOUSE (1936–9)

At Railway Street, a much-delayed scheme called
Liberty House was finally completed in 1939. The site,
formerly a red-light district around Railway Street and
Gloucester Street, was first marked for clearance in 1918
and, after the 1931 Housing Act was passed, 40 acres of
land were acquired in the area. Work finally began on
building two four-storey blocks in 1938, with the blocks
aligning Railway Street and James Joyce Street, and set
around an open square at the back. Although similar
in design to Simms' earlier work, the scheme featured
curved end bays, which incorporated unusual built-in
verandas and eye-catching recessed arched windows
at ground-floor level, flanked by a narrow rectangu-
lar window on either side. Otherwise, the buildings are
typical of mid-period Simms schemes, with a flat roof,
overhanging eaves, a subtle mixture of brick and render
on the facades and rear access via galleries. Rents for
the 181 flats started at 2s a week and were heavily subsidised. When attempts were made to raise the basic rent
to 5s a few years later, the tenants organised a rent strike.

COUNTESS MARKIEVICZ HOUSE (1939)

Later in 1939 came a proposal to build 168 dwellings and twelve shops taking in Townsend Street, Mark Street and Mark's Lane in a U-plan multiple-bay four-storey apartment complex, with modernist flat roofs and over-hanging eaves, to be named Countess Markievicz House. While contemporary European influences are clear, the building remains in sympathy with the street's existing buildings. To enhance this scheme, Simms used simple brick and render details, alternating coloured brick bands and brick detailing on the curved corners and entrance blocks. Block names were picked out in a Celtic typeface. Access to the flats was by stair towers and galleries from an interior courtyard, with the gallery walls in roughcast and the stairs in smooth render. Windows were square in shape with red-brick soldier voussoirs and red-brick sills matching the red-brick balconies. An eye-catching feature was an expressionist-influenced arched entrance, while adding interest were the ground-floor shop units.

MARROWBONE LANE (1930–40)

Marrowbone Lane was a notorious slum in the Cork Street area of the Liberties, with the makeshift buildings in the warren of alleys and lanes containing glue and tannery works, foundries, maltings and even a lace factory as well as the hovels that passed as homes.

Tenders for a block flat scheme on a site backing on to the Guinness brewery were first issued in 1930, with work finally beginning in 1937 and completed just after the start of the Second World War in 1940. Inhabitants of the cleared area were moved to Emmet House at Watling Street.

Plans for the 112-unit flat block to cost £66,152 submitted by Simms to the Corporation's Housing Committee in late 1936 were approved, with E. & W. Dempsey from Castleknock, County Dublin, given the contract to build. Construction began in 1938 and although drawings were made for pram sheds and a play-ground in September 1939, these were held off. When additional land was acquired on favourable terms from Guinness, Simms suggested extending the scheme. Since the Corporation was finding it difficult to acquire sites in slum areas, this was good news.

Like Ballybough House, built in 1939, the Marrowbone Lane flats make up a single long block, punctuated by at least one canted archway entrance to the courtyard behind. At the front, three blocks built with brick and concrete line the street; a set-back middle range breaks up the sheer scale of the frontage. Stripes of red Ballinphellic brick and buff stock, available locally, run the length of the blocks, interrupted only by angular towers of red-brick 'hinges'. Concrete eaves with a gen-erous overhang give the roofs a definite cap. At either end of the main frontage are two beautifully curved corners where the buildings fold back to enclose the courtyard; because of the site's awkward wedge shape, one of the two shorter blocks is longer than the other. With 122 units, the building is large but on a human scale. A high wall at the back marks the boundary with the Guinness site. Mesh reinforcement for concrete was supplied from a local company called McNaughton's Twisteel based on East Wall Road.

Other details include art-deco stairwells and the decks, which came to be described as Dublin's streets in the sky. Each flat had its own door and either a two- or three-window pattern. In a standard layout, two doors at the end of the hall led to the master bedroom and living room, which faced the street side of the building. Off the living room was a small kitchen with built-in units. In a salute both to the Georgian style and to modernist thinking, the windows are generous in size and fill the rooms with light.

Unlike in earlier schemes, the facade is plain, with no individual brick balconies on the street front – perhaps as a concession to wartime shortages but also based on feedback from tenants who rarely used the balconies and regarded them as unnecessary, especially since they blocked light coming into the room behind and also into the room of the flat below.

MARY AIKENHEAD HOUSE (1937–40)

Mary Aikenhead House on Basin Street close to St James's Hospital, completed in 1940 after work began in 1937, is a C-plan four-storey scheme, with the characteristic flat roofs, overhanging eaves, red-brick facade and square windows of Simms' middle style. Set back from the street and railed off, the scheme of 150 flats fits perfectly into its site, with the longest north-facing facade on St James's Street, a shorter range on Basin View and the two joined by a short range which also faces Basin View. Entrance is from Basin Street Lower, with the courtyard and playground almost completely enclosed. Access to the flats is from stairways and decks finished in roughcast render. Its north block includes three shops. Balconies, especially those on the corners, help break down the scale of the large block. A smaller L-shaped block, built in the same style, is located on the other side of Basin Street Lower.

MERCER HOUSE (1929–34)

One of Simms' first projects after arriving back in Dublin was Mercer House in the Crabbe Lane area off Mercer Street Upper behind the Royal College of Surgeons on St Stephen's Green. Work on Mercer House, a four-storey block designed by Horace O'Rourke, had begun in 1929 with H. & J. Martin the contractors. Phase 2, designed by Simms and perhaps Robert Lawrie, began after the purchase of adjoining lands in 1932; it had a classic facade, with access to the flat by an external balcony at the rear. Built in yellow brick with decorative red-brick detail and with a mansard roof on the fourth floor, the block is distinctly Arts and Crafts in style. Of its 104 flats, fifty-six were three-roomed, forty two-roomed and eight four-roomed. The scheme was extended, with Simms the architect, in 1937.

NEWFOUNDLAND STREET/SHERIFF STREET (1948–52)

Tenders for twelve blocks of flats in the Newfoundland Street and Sheriff Street area were issued in 1948, with the contract prepared by Simms. Donald Tyndall, with a private practice based at 121 St Stephen's Green, was named as the supervisory architect.

The site had been cleared and then left for several years. In his site strategy, Simms was clearly influenced by the modernist *Zeilenbau* system, where the long axis of a building was north-south, so that the east front got the morning sun and west front the evening sun, with no frontages facing north. This would prove controversial, since most houses at the time faced south, with the back facing north when possible. In Sheriff Street, situated in a triangle bounded by the docks, the Royal Canal and the railway, the twelve four-storey flat blocks, divided into three sections called St Laurence's Mansions, St Brigid's Gardens and Phil Shanahan House, were built in pairs to form courtyards; each provided 256 flat units.

The 'public' elevations were built in Ballinphellic brick and the block book-ended by towers and corner windows. Windows were grouped in pairs. On the Mayor Street side, two-storeyed shops were used to enclose the first row of courtyards, as at Donore Avenue.

Unfortunately, the blocks faced each other across a wasteland and the scheme, which was close to the city but cut off from it by a 30-foot boundary wall, became a hotbed of antisocial behaviour. With the incorporation of Sheriff Street into the Custom House Docklands scheme in 1987, a decision was made to demolish the flats at a time when 385 of them were still occupied. All 1,000 residents were rehoused and the blocks were demolished in 1998.

NORTH WILLIAM STREET (1947)
Following the 1941 North Strand bombings, a block containing sixteen flats was built and completed in 1947 at North William Street off Summerhill.

OLIVER BOND HOUSE (1936)
Largest by some way of the earlier schemes was the Oliver Bond House development, spread over seven acres of the former Anchor brewery site on Oliver Bond Street, Bridgefoot Street and Usher Street. The former brewery – originally the Bianconi stables – was demolished in May 1933. Winning the contract for a complex of thirteen pitched-roofed buildings in brick and concrete were Meagher & Hayes of Dublin and Cork, with between 600 to 800 men employed on the project. Courtyards on Usher Street and Bridgefoot Street were included in the scheme, with numerous entrances from a road running through the area.

Of the 391 flats eventually completed, with twenty-four in each block, 250 were two-bedroomed, with a scullery, a cooker and a bath with a lid over it acting as the dining table. A further 130 flats had a single bedroom, while four were three-bedroomed and four were single-room bedsits. Entrance to all was at the rear, gallery-style. Also on the site were three houses for live-in caretakers and children's playgrounds. In 1955 the modernist architect Michael Scott was commissioned to design new flats for the estate at Bridgefoot Street. These flats were demolished in 2006.

PEARSE HOUSE (1931–8)

Pearse House, originally planned in 1931, consisted of nine blocks fronting Hanover Street East and running along Sandwith Street Lower, Erne Street Lower and Erne Place Lower. When it was finally completed in 1938, it would provide 345 flats. Building finally started on the art-deco-style complex, with shallow projecting bays and curved corners in 1934 or 1935.

Among the decorative details on the blocks are a stepped centre panel flanked by wings, hinting at the aviation industry, a symbol for a brave new future. An arched entrance with apartments spread over it at first floor level, Amsterdam-style, was adopted. Behind the buildings were a playground, hard landscaped seats and a community sports centre. Like at the Greek Street development, plaster rather than brick was used as a finish.

Built-in flower boxes were incorporated into the decorative projecting balconies for the first time. Some critics, among them Thomas Bodkin, the former National Gallery of Ireland director, believed these might destroy the 'just proportions of a well-designed facade', since tenants had differing taste in flowers.

ST AUDOEN'S HOUSE (1936–41)

St Audoen's House is a single block of fifty-five four-storey flats running along Cook Street and turning the corner onto Bridge Street Lower, with an eye-catching clock tower and entrance. The tower has some fine brick detailing, while the brick-clad ranges feature hipped roofs and access to the flats from the rear courtyard through stair towers and rendered galleries.

ST JOSEPH'S MANSIONS (1936–9)

In November 1936 came a proposal to build a four-block scheme in the garden of Aldborough House on Portland Row, an abandoned Georgian mansion which fell into the hand of the city authorities as early as 1839. In 1935, after the building was acquired by the Post Office, the former garden area – then covered by warehouses – was taken over by Dublin Corporation. Urban legend has it that the site's potential was spotted by Dublin's larger-than-life Lord Mayor, Alfie Byrne, when cycling down Killarney Street. In a state of high excitement, the man sometimes known as the 'shaking hand of Dublin' immediately turned his bicycle in the direction of the Corporation's headquarters. When he arrived, he told officials that he had found a partial solution to the inner city's housing crisis.

Built as a square facing Buckingham Street, Empress Place and Killarney Street on three sides and the rear of Aldborough House on the fourth, the St Joseph's Mansions scheme of 138 flats had pitched roofs and access to the flats through a secure interior courtyard that included a garden and play area. Far from presenting a uniform horizontal face to the public, a facade of two ranges was bookmarked at either end by projecting balconies topped with a traditional roof and chimney stacks. Red brick was used to face the bottom three storeys, with yellow used for the fourth, while an impressively detailed art-deco entrance arch, with narrow vertical windows to each side and a horizontal window over it, led into the rear of the complex.

A modern Child Welfare Clinic and Dining Hall at the development was officially opened by the Lord Mayor Kathleen Clarke on 18 July 1939, when Simms presented Mrs Clarke with a golden key, supplied by the contractors G. & T. Crampton, with which to perform the honours. It was the first centre of its kind to be incorporated into one of the city's housing schemes. Affectionately known as 'Joey's', St Joseph's had a chequered history before it reopened in 2003 as Killarney Court after an €18 million facelift and remodelling. It is managed by the Clúid housing association.

ST MARY'S MANSIONS (1941–2)

Despite serious shortages of both brick and steel during the Second World War, St Mary's Mansions, located between Sean McDermott Street and Railway Street, was completed in 1942 after numerous delays. At the time of the North Strand bombings in 1941, the site had been cleared and, with fears of another bombing and no shortage of concrete, it served as the largest air-raid shelter on the north inner city. Large-scale exercises and bombing raid trial runs took place using the site and the scheme of forty-two flats, with entrances on both streets, was later built over the air-raid shelters. These were extensively refurbished in the 1990s. From 2015 to 2017 the entire scheme, managed by the Clúid housing association, underwent extensive – and controversial – remodelling with existing apartments combined to create larger units and two storeys added to the building, which now provides eighty flats.

ST MICHAN'S HOUSE (1932–4)

After Mercer House came Simms' first solo effort: St Michan's House on Greek Street behind the Bridewell and close to the Four Courts which, since the start of the century, was recognised as one of the city's worst slums. The scheme consisted of two four-storey perimeter blocks of 104 flats, with a plaster rather than a brick finish. Features included sun verandas and baths. It was widely praised and considered as good a design as anything on offer in Berlin, Moscow or Vienna.

ST TERESA'S GARDENS (1940–51)

Like Fatima Mansions, St Teresa's Gardens in Donore Avenue, Rialto was initially designed in the 1930s when the site, previously a large house and gardens called Brook Lawn, was purchased by Dublin Corporation. Simms came up with a plan around 1940 and foundations were poured in 1942, at which point the scarcity of building materials due to the war halted further progress.

Tenders for the construction of twelve four-storey blocks were invited in June 1948, with building beginning soon after and the scheme finally completed in 1951, providing 328 flats as well as ground-floor shops and communal facilities fronting Donore Avenue. Most of the flats had either three or four rooms. Ten terraced houses were built later. As in similar Dutch and British developments, the blocks, built in red brick with little in the way of ornamentation, featured a strong horizontal emphasis, with round windows adding interest. Elements of Simms' original design were modified to cut costs, with the two crescent entrance blocks becoming rectilinear in form and the stair cores, which provided access to the blocks, pared back.

For the overall layout of the scheme, Simms used a *Zeilenbau* arrangement. At the entrance were four aligned blocks marked by curved towers and containing shops. Behind these was an open space, later used for car parking, and lining up behind that were ten identical four-storey blocks. Because the spaces between the flat blocks were neither courtyard nor garden, they became a confused no-man's land. The lack of landscaping and an uncomfortable relationship to the surrounding neighbourhood gave rise to antisocial behaviour, and while two blocks were refurbished, the remaining eight blocks and ten houses were all torn down by 2018, with plans for providing 1,000 homes on the same site.

THORNCASTLE STREET (1936–9)

Looking on to the Dodder river as it enters the Liffey at Grand Canal Docks in Ringsend was the Thorncastle Street flats scheme, originally called Whelan House and O'Rahilly House. Built in three blocks, the first block closest to Bridge Street, dating from 1936, features windows on the curved corners. The less distinguished final block was built in 1939. In total, the scheme provided sixty-four apartments.

B. Urban and Suburban 'Cottage' Schemes 1929–50

Cabra (Faussagh Lane)

1929: roads and sewers constructed
1930: scheme of 641 houses divided into two sections; tenant-purchase scheme completed by October 1931

Marrowbone Lane

1930: 166 cottages; seventeen two-roomed; 138 three-roomed, eleven four-roomed

Donnelly's Orchard, Clonliffe Road (extension)

1932–4: 148 houses; 137 three-roomed, eleven four-roomed.; also upgrade of the original eighty-four tenant-purchase houses built in 1923

Ormond Market

1932–5: nine three-roomed cottages

Malone Gardens, Sandymount

1933: sixty-five cottages; fifty-nine three-roomed; six four-roomed

Cabra Extension Area (Beggsboro)

1933–4: 684 houses in two sections; 596 three-roomed; eighty-eight four-roomed

Friend's (or French) Field, Ballybough

1933–4: 144 houses; 140 three-roomed, four four-roomed

Cabra (Annamoe Road)

1933–4: 311 houses; 297 three-roomed, fourteen four-roomed
1940: 253 houses (Section 1A)

Crumlin (South)
1934: 1,618 houses (Sections 1, 2, 3, 4)
1935: 485 houses (Sections 5 and 7)
1936: 537 houses (Section 6); 275 houses (Sections 8 and 9)
1937: 445 houses (Section 11)
1939: 497 houses (Section 3)
Of the planned 3,583 houses in Crumlin South, 2,903 were built; 1,799 three-roomed and 1,104 four-roomed

North Lotts
1935: 582 houses; 486 three-roomed, ninety-six four-roomed

Cook Street
1936: three four-roomed cottages

South Lotts Road, Ringsend
1937: sixteen houses; fourteen three-roomed, two four-roomed

Harold's Cross
1936–9: 161 houses; eighty-three three-roomed, seventy-eight four-roomed

Terenure
1938: 313 houses; thirty-three three-roomed; 247 four-roomed

Collins Avenue
1938:

Ellenfield
1937: 182 houses (Section 2)
1938: 184 houses (Section 2)
All 327 houses built by 1939 were four-roomed

Larkhill
1938: 537 houses

Emmet Road, Kilmainham
1938–40: sixty-two houses

Crumlin (North)
1939: 353 houses; ninety-two three-roomed; 261 four-roomed

Cabra (West)
1940: 253 four-roomed houses (Section 1A); 250 four-roomed houses (Section 2A); 469 houses (Section 2); 663 houses (Section 3); 250 houses (Section 2A); 332 houses (Section 3A)

Sarsfield Road, Ballyfermot
1947: 203 houses (Section 3)

C. Estates

BALLYFERMOT (1947–64)

Plans for building public housing in Ballyfermot, a suburb located about five miles from Dublin city centre, date back to the mid-1930s, when the area was mostly farmland. In 1947, Dublin Corporation bought a substantial tract of land from Patrick Rafter, and the invitation to tender soon followed for a scheme of 203 houses in the Sarsfield Road Section 3, south of Sarsfield House and Ballyfermot Road. A total of 1,594 houses were eventually built in the Sarsfield Estate, Ballyfermot Lower and Colepark Estate, with the roads named after people, places and battles associated with Patrick Sarsfield. More development followed over the next few decades in the Blackditch, Drumfinn, Cloverhill and Cherry Orchard estates.

CABRA (1929–40)

In Cabra, construction began in 1929 at Faussagh Road. At the time, commissioners were still managing the city and tenant purchase was the favoured option for public housing. After roads and sewers were constructed by John Kenny and Sons, the building of 641 houses began, all four-roomed, in two sections of the area. H. & J. Martin and G. & T. Crampton were the contractors. Names were assigned to the new roads and applications from families of four or more were invited for the new houses. By October 1931, 442 were already occupied.

An extension area, called Beggsboro after the previous landowner George Beggs, was approved in March 1931 by the city manager. Work began in April 1932, soon after Simms' appointment as housing architect. Of the 678 houses approved, 594 were three-roomed and the remaining eighty-four four-roomed. St Jarlath, St Fintan, St Eithne, St Attracta and Annamoe roads were all completed by mid-1934. On 1 June 1933 tenders were invited for the Annamoe Road area on the south side of the site, where roads were built in August 1934. G. & T. Crampton were the contractors.

In 1938 a scheme of 1,950 houses was planned for Cabra West. After compulsory purchase orders were published in 1937, a price was set for the site. Although an extension of the earlier Cabra scheme, Cabra West had distinctive boundaries: the main Cabra Road and the Phoenix Park to the south, railway lines to the north and east, and the Ratoath road to the west, leading the traveller to the Eighth Lock bridge on the Royal Canal. Faussagh Avenue was the main avenue.

Plans for Cabra West were approved in 1940 and the tender for Section 1a was awarded to Fearon – 253 houses at a cost of £118,176 2s 6d, while H. & J. Martin signed up to build 250 houses in Section 2a. Further tenders followed and by the end of 1941, 1,312 houses were ready for their occupants at Carnlough, Dingle, Drumcliffe, Dunmanus, Inver, Ratoath and Swilly roads and on Faussagh Avenue. Houses were built in short terraces, with semi-detached houses featuring at major junctions. Two styles were used; the first featured two windows to the front, a lintel over the door and a coloured course between the storeys. In the second style, used for the terraces, the two central houses had a hip roof at right angles to the main roof. Most houses were finished in concrete render.

Twelve acres were reserved for social and recreational use, with a large green space in the centre of the scheme. Overall, the scheme was designed as a series of concentric roads. Space was allowed for a church, which was the focus of the community, and also for shops. Public houses were not allowed on Corporation estates. A 1.8-hectare site was set aside for industries and in 1945, the Batchelors canning factory opened on Bannow Road to the north of the estate having previously considered building in Santry.

By the end of 1946 when Ventry Drive, Ventry Park, Kilkieran Road, Mulroy Road, Barrow Road, Drumcliffe, Killala Road, Liscannor Road and finally Broombridge Road and Ventry Road were completed, the population of Cabra West had grown from 1,667 in 1936 to 15,556 in the decade following. In total, 22,249 houses were built in Cabra.

CRUMLIN (1934–40)

Proposals for the large estates in Crumlin and Drimnagh had emerged from the first Abercrombie report, published in 1922, where it was described as an 'extra-urban area of 430 acres'; larger than Cabra with 400 acres and the 166 acres at Drumcondra. It would later stretch to almost a thousand acres.

A sewerage system was laid down as early as 1925 to 1929, so Simms inherited this development. The first 247.5 acres (about 110 hectares) at Crumlin South followed compulsory purchase orders in 1934 costing £55,158. Construction began in 1934; by 1939, 3,353 houses were built and by 1950, that number had risen to 5,500. With an urgent need for public housing at the cheapest possible price, Crumlin was built in short terraces to a much more uniform plan than earlier schemes. Most houses had only three rooms, making them far too small for the average family; mindful of this, the Corporation changed its policy and built more four-roomed houses in the later stages of the Crumlin development.

Tenders were invited on 7 March 1934 for 537 houses in Sections 1 and 3, consisting of 223 three-roomed and fifty-nine four-roomed houses. Contractors were warned that they must be prepared, if called up, to erect a further 147 three-roomed and 108 four-roomed houses at Section 3. Just over a month later, on 13 April 1934, tenders were invited for Sections 2 and 4 with 251 three-roomed, and sixty-seven four-roomed houses planned. Again contractors had to be prepared to build a further 191 three-roomed and sixty-four four-roomed houses in Section 4 if called upon. By the summer of 1934, construction of over a thousand two-storey houses in the four sections of what was called Crumlin South was underway.

The next tender issued came on 17 September 1935 for 485 houses in Sections 5 and 7. Of those, 275 would be three-roomed and 210 four-roomed. That was followed by an invitation to tender for 537 houses, 444 of them three-roomed and ninety-three four-roomed, in Section 6 on 11 January 1936 with the warning to contractors that they might be required to build a further fourteen three-roomed and two four-roomed houses at South Lotts Road in Ringsend. Tenders for a further 275 houses in Sections 8 and 9 were invited on 17 April 1936; 206 were three-roomed and sixty-nine four-roomed. Over a year later tenders were invited on 30 August 1937 for forty-four houses in Section 11, all of them four-roomed.

In 1938 work began on 2,416 houses in Crumlin North off Kildare Road, with these completed in 1944 and 1945. A move away from smaller houses continued with almost all the houses having four rooms.

Crumlin, the largest housing development in the Dublin area, consisted of rows of small houses built in blocks of four or eight, with pebble-dash exteriors and details such as lintels and architraves picked out in brick or render or in brick clad with render. A string course marked the division between the ground floor and the first storey. The contractor was G. & T. Crampton. Simms attempted variety by small alterations to the roofline and the placement of houses. For instance, two end-of-terrace houses might be pushed forward with the surrounding houses having a pedimented gable, while corner houses were often built with more elaborate materials.

Crumlin followed a simplified version of the garden-suburb ideal, most notably at Clonmacnoise Road, where culs-de-sac and crescents radiated from a central circular park in a Celtic cross formation and the roads were named after monastic settlements. The houses themselves, compact yet functional, were built to three standard designs with a living room, including a prefabricated fireplace, at the front along with a small hall and stairway and a kitchen and bathroom at the back. Larger houses included a 'parlour' used for entertaining guests. Upstairs were two or three bedrooms off a small landing. The largest bedroom was to the front over the living room, with a second fireplace to keep it warm.

Details such as the 'swing' of the doors were carefully considered by Simms and his team. High-quality skirting boards, doors, architraves, floorboards, stairs and handrails made in the Crampton workshops added the finishing touches indoors, as did meticulously-designed gates and railings outdoors.

When the first phase of the Crumlin scheme was completed in 1940, almost 3,000 new houses were ready for occupation; 1,803 of them were three-roomed and 1,172 four-roomed. On 30 September 1940, 2,064 of a planned 2,492 dwellings were completed in Crumlin North.

From 4,000 in 1936, Crumlin's population had risen to 34,111 a decade later, making it by some way the largest housing development in the country.

DONNELLY'S ORCHARD (1923–34)

One of the first schemes where an outside contractor undertook the road and sewer construction work was Donnelly's Orchard, on a site between Clonliffe Road and the Tolka river where eighty-four red-brick tenant-purchase houses, all with five rooms, were completed in 1923.

Between 1932 and 1934 a further 148 houses were built on the site, all of them smaller; 137 were three-roomed and eleven four-roomed, while the original houses were upgraded to include baths and hot water services.

DONNYCARNEY (1929–48)

When a site of just over 31 acres off Collins Avenue was acquired by Dublin Corporation in 1928, Donnycarney was still considered a rural area, well outside the city's central hub.

By July 1929 Dublin Corporation was considering nine tenders for a tenant-purchase scheme of 434 four-roomed houses at prices of between £300 and £380. Section 1 originally consisted of 255 houses with this reduced to 242 when it was decided to retain the tennis courts on the site. Awarded the contract was John Kenny and Sons. Estimated cost was £92,102 17s 11d, with the scheme to be completed in forty-five weeks. Winning the contract for Section 2, consisting of 179 houses to be built in fifty-two weeks at a cost of £67,086 12s 2½d, was the Housing Corporation of Great Britain.

By February 1931 a hundred houses remained to be completed by Kenny, who aimed to have them ready for occupation by April. In the end, 421 houses were completed on a grid-like layout, with a 'circus' bisected by Elm Road and Oak Road, and a number of culs-de-sac off Donnycarney Road. The houses were finished in the standard pebble dash, although the semi-detached houses placed at angles to the road at junctions received special treatment, with red roof tiles rather than the black slate used in the other houses and mock-Tudor timber detailing on the upper storey.

With the roads and sewers complete, a new scheme of rental housing was planned starting with Clanawley Road, where fifty-four houses were built in 1948, followed by Clanburgh, Clanmahon, Clanree, Clanranald, Collins Avenue East, Kilbride and Killester Avenue and later by Clanboy, Clancarthy, Clanmaurice, Clonmoyle, Clandonagh and Malahide Road. Along its length, from Whitehall at one end to the Howth Road at the other, Collins Avenue was built piecemeal, with houses at junctions the first to be built and areas then allowed to develop.

ELLENFIELD (1937–9)

On 3 December 1937 tenders were invited for 182 houses and recreation park boundaries at Ellenfield Section 2 in the heart of Whitehall, a site bordered by the Swords Road, Collins Avenue West and Beaumont Road. On 7 February 1938 tenders were again invited for the same scheme and, in the end, the Corporation decided to build the estate itself using direct labour supervised by a works manager. While the quality of the work was good, the scheme took longer to build and using its own labour proved more costly for the Corporation.

When completed in 1939, Ellenfield consisted of about 327 houses, all but one four-roomed; the remaining house had five rooms. It was a relatively small and self-contained estate, with easy access to main roads and the minimum of through traffic. As in Crumlin, houses were built in short terraces of up to six houses, with semi-detached houses at junctions. Most of the houses were rendered in concrete and had tiled roofs, except on the main road, where the houses were faced with red brick.

Although there was no particular provision for cars, the Ellenfield roads were wider and a significant amount of green space was included in the scheme as well as good-sized gardens front and rear. To the north-west of the development was a park bordering the grounds of the large Catholic church.

EMMET ROAD (1938–40)

On 22 June 1938 tenders were sought for sixty-two four-room houses and a children's playground at a site between Emmet Road and Bulfin Road, between Inchicore and Kilmainham. Nothing much happened for the next two years and tenders were again invited on 2 March 1940.

FRIEND'S FIELD (1933–4)

Friend's Field on Clonliffe Road was also known as French Field, and as Mud Island during the land reclamation project of the nineteenth century. Between 1933 and 1934, 144 houses were built, with 140 of them three-roomed and four four-roomed, on a site to the south of Clonliffe Road near the Croke Park stadium. Donnelly's Orchard was on the other side of Clonliffe Road and both estates were close to Poplar Row, where Ballybough House was later built.

HAROLD'S CROSS (1936–9)

A plan for building 161 houses – eighty-three three-roomed, seventy-eight four-roomed – was subject to an inquiry in 1936. With modifications, the houses were built by 1939.

LARKHILL (1936–41)

For the Larkhill estate, almost across the road from Ellenfield on the Swords Road, tenders were sought for 537 four-roomed houses and an estate-office annexe on 1 April 1938. Larkhill was an oblong development with access from

Collins Avenue West. As at Ellenfield, the houses were built in short terraces of varying length. To add variety, the middle two houses in a terrace were stepped forward.

NORTH LOTTS (1934–5)

At the North Lotts, off East Wall Road, a neat development of 582 cottages was built in 1935, with 486 of them three-roomed and ninety-six four-roomed.

SOUTH LOTTS (1937)

A small development of sixteen houses was built by 1937; fourteen of them were three-roomed and the remaining two were four-roomed.

TERENURE (1936–52)

After acquiring a 42-acre site in 1936, Dublin Corporation invited tenders in early January 1937 for a scheme of 309 houses in the Terenure area, consisting of seventy three-roomed and 239 four-roomed dwellings; carriageways, pathways and sewers were also required. After objections from ratepayers in nearby Mayfield Road, Eaton Square, Terenure Park and Ashdale Road, the Corporation agreed that 40 per cent of the housing would be of 'a better type'. A Guinness offer to buy 22 acres of the site off Mount Tallant Avenue and build houses with four or more rooms, plus kitchen and bathroom, was accepted, with the first sod turned in January 1949. Builders were Alexander Hill and Company. The cost of each house was £1,950 with a government and corporation grant of £350 per house. The first house was occupied on 8 August 1949. By the early 1950s, when the development was completed, 238 such houses were built, most of them on Corrib Road, each with three bedrooms, a large living room, separate kitchen, bathroom and gardens front and rear. The estate also boasted a playground, a football ground and its own caretaker.

Bibliography and Sources

Books

Aalen, F.H.A. and Kevin Whelan (eds), *Dublin City and County: From Prehistory to Present* (Dublin,1992)

—, *The Iveagh Trust: The First Hundred Years 1890–1990* (Dublin, 1990)

Abercrombie, Patrick, Sydney A. Kelly and Arthur J. Kelly, *Dublin of the future: the new town plan, being the scheme awarded first prize in the international competition* (Liverpool, 1922)

Abercrombie, Patrick, et al., *Sketch Development Plan for Dublin* (1941)

Bannon, Michael J. (ed.), *The Emergence of Irish Planning 1800–1920* (Dublin, 1985)

—, (ed.), *Planning: The Irish Experience 1920–1988* (Dublin, 1989)

Brady, Joseph, *Dublin, 1930–1950: The Emergence of the Modern City* (Dublin, 2014)

—, *Dublin, 1950–1970: Houses, Flats and High Rise* (Dublin, 2016)

—, *Dublin in the 1950s and 1960s: Cars, Shops and Suburbs* (Dublin, 2017)

—, and Ruth McManus, *Building Healthy Homes: Dublin Corporation's First Housing Schemes, 1880–1925* (Dublin, 2021)

Brown, Terence, *Ireland: A Social and Cultural History, 1922–1985* (London, 1985)

Cameron, Charles, *How the Poor Live* (Dublin, 1904)

—, *A Brief History of Municipal Public Health Administration in Dublin* (Dublin, 1914)

Casey, Christine, *Dublin: The City Within the Grand and Royal Canals and the Circular Road with the Phoenix Park* (New Haven and London, 2005)

Clark, Mary, and Gráinne Doran, *Serving the City: The Dublin City Managers and Town Clerks 1230–1996* (Dublin City Council, 2006)

Cullen, Paul, *With a Little Help from My Friends: Planning Corruption in Ireland* (Dublin, 2002)

Daly, Mary E., *Dublin the Deposed Capital* (Cork, 1984)

Davitt, M., *The Fall of Feudalism in Ireland or, The Story of the Land League Revolution* (London and New York, 1904)

Engels, F., *The Condition of the Working Class in England* (London, 1987)

Fahey et al., *Social Housing in Ireland: A Study of Success, Failure and Lessons Learned* (Dublin, 1999)

Frampton, Kenneth, *Modern Architecture: A Critical History* (London, 2020)

Fraser, M., *John Bull's Other Homes: State Housing and British Policy in Ireland, 1883–1922* (Liverpool, 1996)

Geddes, Patrick, *Cities in Evolution: An introduction to the town planning movement and to the study of civics* (London, 1915)

Hanlon, Bernadette, and Thomas J. Vicino (eds), *The Routledge Companion to the Suburbs* (London, 2018)

Hanna, Erika, *Modern Dublin: Urban Change and the Irish Past, 1957–1973* (Oxford, 2013)

Kearns, Kevin C., *Dublin Tenement Life: An Oral History* (Dublin, 1994)

Kenna, Padraic, *Housing Law, Rights and Policy* (Dublin, 2011)

Lee, J.J., *Ireland 1912–1985* (Cambridge, 1989)

MacLaran, Andrew, *Dublin: The Shaping of a Capital* (London, 1993)

McCabe, Conor, *Sins of the Father: Tracing the Decisions that Shaped the Irish Economy* (Dublin, 2013)

McDermott, Matthew J., *Dublin's Architectural Development 1800–1925* (Dublin, 1988)

McDonald, Frank, *Saving the City: How to Halt the Destruction of Dublin* (Dublin, 1989)

—, *The Construction of Dublin* (Dublin, 2000)

—, *A Little History of the Future of Dublin* (Dublin, 2021)

McManus, Ruth, *Dublin 1910–1940* (Dublin, 2002)

Meghen, P.J., *Housing in Ireland* (Dublin, 1965)

Pfretzschner, Paul A., *The Dynamics of Irish Housing* (Dublin, 1965)

Plunkett, James, *Strumpet City* (London, 1969)

Potter, Matthew, *The Municipal Revolution in Ireland: A Handbook of Urban Government in Ireland since 1800* (Dublin, 2011)

O'Brien, Joseph V., *Dear Dirty Dublin: A City in Distress 1899–1916* (Berkeley, 1982)

Ó Broin, Leon, *Dublin Castle and the 1916 Rising* (New York, 1971)

O'Connell, Cathal, *The State and Housing in Ireland: Ideology, Policy and Practice* (New York, 2007)

Ó Gráda, Diarmuid, *Georgian Dublin: The Forces That Shaped the City* (Cork, 2015)

O'Leary, Seán, *Sense of Place: A History of Irish Planning* (Dublin, 2014)

Ó Maitiú, S., *Dublin's Suburban Towns 1834–1930* (Dublin, 2002)

O'Neill, Ciaran (ed.), *Irish Elites in the 19th Century* (Dublin, 2013)

Robertson, Manning, *A Cautionary Guide to Dublin* (Dublin, 1934)

—, *The Handbook of National Planning and Reconstruction* (Dublin, 1944)

Rothery, Sean, *Ireland and the New Architecture 1900–1940* (Dublin, 1989)

Rowley, Ellen (ed.), *More than Concrete Blocks Vol. 1 1900–40* (Dublin, 2016)

—, *More than Concrete Blocks Vol. 2 1940–72* (Dublin, 2018)

—, *Housing, Architecture and the Edge Condition: Dublin is building, 1935–1975* (London, 2018)

Tyrwhitt, Jaqueline (ed.), *Patrick Geddes in India* (London, 1947)

Warburton, John, James Whitelaw and Robert Walsh, *History of the City of Dublin: From the Earliest Accounts to the Present Time* (London, 1818)

Wright, Myles, *Final Report and Advisory Plan for the Dublin Region* (Dublin, 1967)

Yeates, Pádraig, *A City in Wartime: Dublin 1914–1918* (Dublin, 2011)

—, *A City in Turmoil: Dublin 1919–1921* (Dublin, 2012)

—, *A City in Civil War: Dublin 1921–1924* (Dublin, 2015)

Articles/Papers

By Herbert Simms

Simms, Herbert, 'Municipal Housing Activities in Dublin', Centenary Celebration of the Royal Institute of the Architects of Ireland and Conference of the Royal Institute of British Architects, 21–24 June 1939, RIAI (Dublin, 1939)

By others

Bannon, Michael J., 'Dublin town planning: Ashbee and Chettle's "New Dublin – a study in Civics"' (*Planning Perspectives*, Vol. 14, 1999, Issue 1.0)

—, 'The making of Irish geography III: Patrick Geddes and the emergence of modern town planning in Dublin' (*Irish Geography*, Vol. 11, 1978, Issue 1)

Cullen, Frank, 'The provision of working and lower middle class housing in late nineteenth century urban Ireland' (*Proceedings of the RIA: Archaeology, Culture, History, Literature*, Vol. 111C, Special Issue: Domestic Life in Ireland [00]), pp. 217–51

Downs, Mary, and Martin Medina, 'A Short History of Scavenging' (*Comparative Civilizations Review*, Vol. 42, No. 42, article 4, 2000)

Kennedy, Finola, 'Public Expenditure in Ireland on Housing in the Post-war Period' (*Economic and Social Review*, Vol. 3, No. 3, 1972), pp. 373–401

Killen, James, and Andrew MacLaran (eds), 'Dublin: Contemporary Trends and Issues for the Twenty-first Century' (Geographical Society of Ireland in association with the Centre for Urban and Regional Studies, Trinity College Dublin, 1999)

McManus, Ruth, 'Suburbanisation in Dublin: a Focus on Dublin' in Bernadette Hanlon and Thomas J. Vicino (eds), *The Routledge Companion to the Suburbs* (London, 2018)

Murphy, Frank, 'Dublin Slums in the 1930s' (*Dublin Historical Record*, Vol. 37, No. 3/4 (Jun–Sept 1984), pp. 104–11

New Monthly Magazine and Literary Journal, Vol. III, No. 18 (1822), pp. 503–11

Theses

Conroy, Eddie, 'No Rest for Twenty Years: H.G. Simms and the Problem of Slum Clearance in Dublin' (MA thesis, University College Dublin, 1997)

Crisp, Alan, 'The Working-Class Owner-Occupied House of the 1930s' (MLitt thesis, University of Oxford, 1998)

Public Reports

Dublin Disturbances Commission: Minutes of Evidence and Appendices, HMSO (London, 1914)

Report of Inquiry into the Housing of the Working Classes in the City of Dublin 1939–43 (Dublin, 1943)

Newspapers

Evening Herald
Freeman's Journal
Irish Independent
The Irish Times

Websites

archive.org
openlibrary.org
archiseek.com
turtlebunbury.com
comeheretome.com
databases.dublincity.ie/burgesses/about.php
irishlabourhistorysociety.com

archiseek.com/discussion/topic/the-great-1930s-scheme
dia.ie/architects/view/4969/simms-herbertgeorge
theirishstory.com

Acknowledgements

This book came about largely through conversations with my sister-in-law Cecilia, who had worked on some of the Simms buildings, and my brother David, both of them architects.

David, like me, grew up in an area of Dublin close to the Liffeyside quays. The Benburb Street flats and the warren of streets off Arbour Hill and North Circular Road were part of our local landscape.

Other buildings like the Oliver Bond flats, the clock tower on St Audoen's House and the Iveagh Trust buildings in the Liberties would also catch the eye when we wandered further afield. Later again, the style and quality of the Henrietta Street flats, Ballybough House, and the Pearse and Countess Markievicz developments in the city centre struck home.

The questions began: who had designed these buildings, so much part of the Dublin cityscape yet largely ignored because they were 'Corporation flats'? Unlike more recent developments, they compared well in their design with anything to be seen in London, Paris, Vienna or Amsterdam.

These substantial buildings are now well over seventy years in existence and they need upgrading and attention if they are to survive. Much work has already been done, most notably on Killarney Court (the former 'Joeys'), which now has gorgeous black window frames fitting in perfectly with its Arts and Crafts look. Chancery Court and its neat garden right beside the Four Courts is also well looked after; Pearse House is next for extensive refurbishment.

Plans for these and other buildings had long been lost, making the job of the Dublin City Council architects a lot tougher. Then, miracle of miracles, a stash of the plans was found, bought as part of a job loft by a habitual auction attendee who put them away in the loft of his shed and forgot all about them. Much later, these were discovered by his son when clearing the shed. In 2021 the plans were presented to the Irish Architectural Archive. Cecilia and I would like to thank the IAA staff for letting us spend hours examining the plans and taking photographs. Thank you also to UCD's digital library and to G. & T. Crampton for allowing us use archive photographs.

Thanks also go to the always helpful staff at the National Library of Ireland and to our local library in Blackrock; to all at New Island Books, most notably Djinn von Noorden, Des Doyle and Aoife K. Walsh; and to my agent, Jonathan Williams, for his unwavering support and scrupulous attention to detail.

We hope that, with the help of this book, Dubliners will become more familiar with the Simms buildings and ensure that they survive – at least – for the 200 years, as promised by their architect.

Index